Choose only Love

The Holy Dwelling

BOOK V

Messages from A Choir of Angels
Received by Sebastián Blaksley

TAKE HEART PUBLICATIONS

Elige solo el amor | Choose Only Love

Publication in English authorized by
Fundación amor vivo, a nonprofit organization, Argentina
Av. Libertador 16434
San Isidro
Buenos Aires, Argentina
www.fundacionamorvivo.org

TAKE HEART PUBLICATIONS

13315 Buttermilk Bend
North San Juan, CA 95960
www.takeheartpublications.com
ISBN 978-1-58469-687-2
Cover and editorial design by Alejandro Arrojo
Computer production by   ·
Patty Arnold, *Menagerie Design and Publishing*
Manufactured in the United States of America
May, 2021

Choose only Love

The Holy Dwelling

Table of contents

How It Originated

On October 3, 2018, a presence that was all love and whose magnificence, beauty, and benevolence cannot be described, came to me suddenly in a way I had never before experienced. I understood with perfect clarity that it was the glorious Archangel Raphael. He introduced himself saying, "I am the medicine of God." He told me to pray a particular prayer for nine days. Through inner inspiration he also dictated certain intentions for me to pray. The prayers consisted of five Our Fathers, five Hail Marys, and five Glories, just as these prayers are presented in the Catholic Church, to which I belong.

On October 13, the day after finishing this novena of prayer, I began to receive glorious visits from a choir of countless angels of God accompanied by Archangel Raphael and Archangel Gabriel. Their love and beauty were indescribable. Through the choir came the Voice of Christ, expressed in an ineffable form and as images, shown in symbols visible to the spirit. I put the meaning of these images into written words, then voice recordings.

Each visitation was the same: First I received the images and heard the music that the choir presents, then the chorus departed but Archangels Raphael and Gabriel remained as custodians, or loving presences, until the message or session in question was transcribed.

The glorious Archangel Raphael is the one who guided me in the transcription, assuring that the message is properly received and that what was shown can be passed from image to word. Archangel Gabriel is the loving custodian of everything that concerns the work, not only in reference to the manifestation itself and to the writings, but to everything that arises and will arise from them.

The messages, or sessions, are shown to me as a picture of great beauty in which each form (which has no form) is in itself a voice, a "sound-image." What I hear is like the rhythmical twanging of a harp that becomes translated into words. This tune is a vibration of celestial music whose frequency is unlike the sounds of the world. It is a kind of "vibration-frequency" that the soul knows perfectly well and that I recognize with certainty as the voice of the Lamb of God. Once everything is transcribed in written and spoken words, then the chorus arrives in all its glory once again, as if they were coming to seek the most holy Archangels Raphael and Gabriel. Then all together they retire, singing a hosanna to the Christ of God.

That hosanna sung by the choir of angels is a majestic song of praise and gratitude to the Creator for the infinite mystery of love that is the Second Coming. It is a prelude to His coming. If humankind were able to understand in all its magnitude the ineffable mystery of love that is the Second Coming of Christ, we would eternally sing the mercies of God in union with all the angels.

In cases where the Virgin Mary Herself or Jesus Christ are present in Their human and divine person and communicate directly, the choir of angels is muted with love, in a silence that is sacred. Pure expectation, so to speak, surrounds their blessed presences. The angels bow their heads, cast their eyes downward, and are caught up in an ecstasy of love, veneration, and contemplation. Nothing and no one dares, nor could, interrupt the holy silence in which the universe is submerged before the sovereign presence of Mary and Jesus when They speak directly to our souls. This is because that space of dialogue between Christ and the soul is inviolable. It is the sacred temple of the intimacy of the soul with God.

When Archangel Raphael makes himself present to me and begins the process of translating images and symbols into written words, my will is fused into one will with Him. We are one and the same will. There is no "you" and "me." And yet, even in that unity, there is the consciousness that I am I, and He is He: two persons with the same will, the same consciousness of being, in a single holy purpose. My thinking mind is silenced in this absorption of my being into the Being of all true being, which we share as a unit. My consciousness and His become one. What the will one says to be done, is done. There is no distance between the "be done" and its effect.

The rest of my humanity responds humbly. There is no resistance. There is only a flow of words coming from the Mind of Christ, as if it were from a spring that flows from the top of a mountain. This torrent of Grace made into words makes my fingers fly with speed and precision that far surpasses that of my ordinary writing. The soul remains ecstatic with love and with a single desire—to remain forever fused with the beloved Christ, being of our being and of all true being.

During the visitations my whole being is bathed in great peace and joy, like being embraced by universal love. But after the concentration of putting the message into words, the body shows great fatigue. It seems that it is difficult for it to sustain the energy I receive. The part of the manifestation that includes the chorus of angels, the voice, and the images is something that can happen at any time, place, or in any circumstance. However, the transcription of the symbols received into written words and then spoken and recorded can be delayed until I can make myself available to do so. It may be immediately afterwards or several days later.

The main message of this work could be summarized as follows: The time for a new humanity has arrived, a humanity that is ready to manifest the living Christ in each of us. We are, each of us, Christ. This is the truth about us, even if we perceive ourselves differently. We are already prepared to be able to live life in the certainty that says: I no longer live, but it is Christ who lives in me. Helping us to realize this truth in our lives, here and now, is what this manifestation is about. All of Heaven will help us in this holy purpose, since it is the Second Advent itself.

A Description of the Manifestations

When the Archangels come, they come without wings. They are like humans wearing tunics. Raphael's tunic is green, edged with gold. Gabriel's tunic is pink, almost white, edged with yellow. Both tunics are majestic, appearing as if made of a very precious silk.

Their faces are cheerful and radiant, with very light yellowish skin. Both have shoulder-length, golden blond hair and their eyes are green. They each have unique facial features. Their bodies are radiant with serene glowing light that generates peace and a great sense of beauty and harmony.

Many of the angels in the Chorus of Angels have light pink and light blue tunics. Others have light gold, but all are pastel colors, again with a serene luminosity. A few have green robes as if they were emeralds but a little lighter.

The permanent happiness that angels exhibit is remarkable. Everything is joy with them. One day they told me that they radiate perpetual happiness because they always share happiness.

The angels are always surrounded by white and majestic light, as if they live in an eternal midday of love and light. They are accompanied by music, as though a celestial choir is singing in all corners of the universe, like the sound of millions of harps playing in unison, forming a harmonious symphony of great beauty.

The angelic vibrations are of such a degree that they calm the mind and the heart, and give peace. One knows, without knowing how, that this vibration is simultaneously prayer and praise. Each part of the universe (creation) sings a song of gratitude for it having been called into existence, as though it has music inside that is a prayer to the Creator. The soul had stopped hearing this celestial music but will begin to hear it again when it returns to the Father's house. Though forgotten, this song is forever loved by souls that love the Father and Creator.

The ineffable, inexpressible beauty of these visions of angels and archangels, submerges the soul in an ecstasy of love and rapture in which one's whole being participates. No joy or happiness on Earth compares with the ecstasy that a vision of the greatness, magnanimity, and beauty of the angels and archangels generates.

Angelic intelligence is of such a degree that it surpasses all worldly understanding. Their thoughts occur at an indescribable speed, even faster than human thought. Without distortion of any kind, their thoughts are pure, without contradiction, with perfect clarity, and express only holiness. As lightning crosses the firmament, so too do angelic thoughts pass through my mind.

I clearly perceive the difference between human thought and thought from the Wisdom of Heaven, due to the way I experience them. Thoughts from Heaven feel like light and breath; they are full of certainty, can never be forgotten, and bring a great "amount" of truth in the blink of an eye. In an instant I understand the full meaning of each manifestation that comes to me.

Humility, prudence, and simplicity are central features of the angels. Their greatest joy is to serve God by being servants of all creation. They love human beings, animals, plants, stones, the elements, and every material and immaterial aspect of creation with a love and tenderness that, when experienced, is capable of melting even the hardest heart.

While the beauty and magnanimity of angelic visions are indescribable, they are a pale flash compared to the magnificence of those of Jesus and Mary. Nothing in the universe resembles the eternal, unnameable beauty of the hearts of Jesus and Mary. They are God Himself made man and woman. They are the joy of the angels and have the veneration of creation. From Them springs all harmony, greatness, and holiness.

The looks of Jesus and Mary, radiating such tenderness and love, melt the entire universe. Their smiles are purity itself. In Their presence the soul is entranced in an ecstasy of veneration and contemplation, leaving it speechless. The soul exhales a moan of joy that says something like *Ah!* For me personally, contemplating the looks and smiles of Jesus and Mary is Heaven.

I hope you can understand what I'm trying to say as I try to describe the indescribable. I only say what I see, hear, and experience. Heaven exists, God exists, and God is love. This is what was given to me to see, hear, and understand.

I hope with all my heart that those who receive this manifestation let themselves be the beloved of God, more and more every day; and in this way be transformed by the beauty of a love that has no beginning or end.

With love in Christ,
Sebastián Blaksley,
A Soul in Love
Buenos Aires, Argentina
January, 2019 and October, 2020

Prelude

A message from Jesus

Beloved of my soul! You are the delight of my heart. Your sweetness is like a balm of reverie in which the universe is submerged in an ecstasy of love and contemplation. You are the delirium of a God who is infinite goodness and beauty beyond compare.

A new hymn of praise and gratitude in honor of your beauty begins as angels sing a symphony in the Kingdom where the light shines eternally.

Oh, ecstasy of the seraphim! Sacred song! Glass of wisdom where is poured the nectar of divinity! Refuge of Holy Love! I live in you since before time began. Love flutters and sighs in you forever.

I am what sustains the universe and what gives brilliance to the light of the world, what makes the sun shine and all luminescence be born. I am the pure intelligence of love. I am the sweetness of the Christ who lives in you. I am a miracle. I am the Word. I am all that is holy, beautiful, perfect. I am one with you.

Soul in love and lover, remain in me as I remain in you. Together we will make the light that never goes out shine brightly until the Earth is alight with our love. Immerse yourself in the mystery of creation. From our union will arise new infinite universes in which only peace will dwell without beginning or end, love without barriers, Divine Love, the love of holiness.

Before the world existed, you and I were.

Before time began and also established an end to time, we were.

Before thought arose, we were.

Together we are the eternity of love. We are the light that shines everywhere. We are an infinite ocean of wisdom and truth. We are the holy dwelling. We are the sweetness of love extending infinitely.

Together we traverse all universes, creating stars and worlds, holy lovers playing a game of beautiful love.

Oh, child of my bosom! Beloved of my being! Every day let us start anew, full of love and kindness. Let my sweetness embrace you, my beauty envelop you, and the light of my glory penetrate your being so that we may give birth to new love every morning, every evening, and every night.

Because of our union, a bird with a wounded wing will regain the majesty of flight. A broken heart will sing again. And from a spring that was dry, the water of eternal life will again flow.

You and I, united forever in love, are one soul, one holy heart, one single being. Together we are the holy dwelling where our beauty shines eternally with a radiance greater than the sun. We are the source of light and life.

Together we are the sweetness of love.

1.

The Name of God

A message from Jesus

I. Symbols and Expression

Soul in love! Here we are again, reunited in the presence of sweet love. I thank you for answering the call from On High. Thank you for receiving me in your heart.

These words are full of love. Absorb them. Make them yours. Let their power transform you.

I am the light that comes from the Father and manifests in you. I am one with you. I am where you aim to be.

Before going further into the sweetness of love it is important to remember that names, like words, have no meaning of their own in the realm of Divine Truth. Remember that love has no words. Nevertheless, in the plane of perception, words can mean a lot. In this work we have deliberately used names with a high emotional content, words endowed with many meanings over the centuries, such as Jesus, Mary, Holy Spirit, God, and many others. Some may consider this to be contradictory.

The laws of perception cannot be evaded while you are ruled by them. Nor need you do so. The love of God does not skip anything you have created in your world. Rather, love joins it, and from that union transforms it, together with you, so that the truth freely shines from behind every word.

This work does not seek converts or followers, or to evangelize a wisdom that others do not know. If this were the goal, this work would be meaningless because it would try to teach what everyone knows: love.

So that this work comes to light, we have selected names and a context for multiple reasons, many of which exceed the purpose of these writings. The essential reason is that of the healing of memory and the reinforcement of your true identity.

Everything could be summarized as a matter of identity. There is a risk when you decide, more or less consciously, to travel the spiritual path. The risk is that of losing identity or creating an identity that is a composite of many spiritual currents—a kind of spiritual hybrid that does not help sustain you within your true identity. Worse, it can increase your confusion and make it more difficult for you to resolve your identity crisis.

I do not advocate confusion, but certainty. And I do not advocate an amorphous identity without a solid anchor.

II. Diversity and Uniqueness

A great challenge in spiritual life, as in every way of life, is to remain totally yourself without losing the flexibility that the universality of love demands. The whole does not annul any part, nor does it need to. The part—you—can be who you want to be.

The names chosen in this work may cause controversy among some and even cause some to reject it. Even that is in accord with the purpose of these writings. Resistance to the word "God" or similar words often reflects a lack of forgiveness or an inability to accept differences. Achieving an open mind and a broad heart that can accommodate everyone equally is part of the goal of this gift of written words from Heaven.

To reject this work because of the names that appear here is like rejecting it because its prose does not seem exalted. That would be staying on the surface. Nevertheless, in certain cases this or similar responses are inevitable and necessary.

Everyone who approaches these writings will experience what love wants them to experience. Everything will come to light and imbibe its sweetness in due time.

To you who receive these words, let me address some things before moving on. It is not you who have come to me but I have come to you. It was not you who chose to read these words, rather they have been looking for you from all eternity.

These words were written in the Heaven of your holy mind and have been calling you ever since. They are not simply letters written on paper or words said and captured on a recording device. They are pure love. They are drops of dew falling on your mind and into your heart to allow your soul to germinate the beauty that you are and bear abundant fruit—the fruit of light and holiness, the fruit of truth and love.

III. Beyond Words

Do not stop at certain words. Refrain from being angry with your past experience with the names of God. Absorb them with the heart. Let them be your guide. Remember that I told you that where you found separation you will now find unity.

Feel how much love the Creator, who has the kindness to write to you, has for you. Long have you been waiting for doors to the Love of Loves to open, and to live more deeply in the holiness that you really are.

These words are a testimony of God's love for you who are His delight. You are a holy, pure, perfect soul. You are as lovely as a beautiful snowflake but without its coldness. You are the living expression of Divine Love.

This work is a diploma for you who have concluded the search for the spiritual life. You have reached the point where you can begin to live as the incarnated Christ you are.

You are Christ. You are what I once was and proved to be two thousand years ago. Now the time has come for you to prove it.

Do not be deterred by symbols. Throughout this work you have experienced much. You have changed greatly, even in ways you cannot yet understand. Your heart knows who is speaking.

Perhaps some part of your mind is still reluctant to believe this call, claiming that you are not worthy to be Christ. No matter. All that is past. Keep going. You know me more than you know yourself because I know you more than you could imagine. I know very well who you are, and why and for what I have chosen you among the multitude.

You are a soul chosen to let the light of Christ shine in the world in which you wish to be. Your past choices do not matter. All that matters is that you live in truth. And this is the truth: you no longer live but Christ lives in you. And you are called to make this truth the center of your existence.

Christ does not care what you call him, nor what associations you make about him. Christ does not have an identity problem. He knows who he is. Neither will you stop at such insignificant matters as whether the name of God is this or that, or whether such and such is the right spiritual path. Those are matters for spiritual children. You are no longer a spiritual child. You are the living Christ who lives in you.

You may think that replacing the word "God" with "being" or "love" would resolve the issue of God's name and associations. But that is incorrect. Every word is charged with emotion and triggers some kind of reaction. What for some is a sign of inclusion for others can be a sign of exclusion.

I am not only addressing those who would reject the names for the Divine used here but also those who have mental idols that would separate rather than unite.

It is a misunderstanding to believe that God gave the truth to some and would have them monopolize it and build institutions. It is part of the thinking pattern of the child that you once were but that must now be left behind.

Everything coming from love unites. What brings about disunity comes from nothing. God is love, and therefore is perfect inclusion.

You can transcend names and forms, and fill them with true uniting love in one way or another.

I am not calling you to do anything in particular, nor to live in any special way, nor to change the world. This is a much more radical call—the call to be fully you as God knows you.

To be as God created you is what I have been talking about all along, for two thousand years. I do it in a multitude of different ways and I will not rest until my voice is heard in every corner of the universe.

This work is the ringing of the Lord's bell. It is the call for which you have been waiting. It is the call to follow what the wisdom of love tells you, so that she, and only she, is the source of your knowledge and action.

This work is prompted by wisdom not of the world. It is the voice of Christ speaking within you in a way that only you can recognize.

It is important to begin to realize that the only relevant thing in you is your direct relationship with your Creator. Be aware that by going through this work together we are growing in the degree of knowledge of our love relationship. It is at this level where this work makes sense. It is in our direct relationship, in the relationship you have with these words and, with them, the Christ who lives in you, wherein lies the power of this work to transform your life.

As you join in peace with your being all the days of your life and remain there in every moment, you will be creating a new Heaven and a new Earth. Do this and you will have returned to love.

2.

The Meeting Point

A message from Jesus

I. Prelude

Sons and daughters of eternity! Many have been looking to meet their brothers and sisters without truly doing so. It seems that something always emerges that separates—a discussion, a point of view, a desire, a belief. Almost anything seems able to disunite sisters and brothers around the world.

Unity, it seems, is so fragile that it is always on the verge of breaking down, or at least is so difficult that it resembles an ideal more than a reality. The reality of love seems alien.

Yet if we continue to live life without managing to live consciously and forever in unity, almost nothing has been achieved on the spiritual path. True spirituality is that which comes from love; it leads you to love more. Everything else is past. We have already noted this.

Unity is not possible if you do not love diversity. Remember, life is diversity. No being is identical to another. Even you are not the same from minute to minute. Everything changes. And yet you are immutable as created by God. How can both realities be reconciled? Immutable and yet constant change? Unity and yet diversity? They seem to be irreconcilable. But they are not.

To live in union it is necessary to recognize that what is one can simultaneously be different. Think of the Earth that your blessed feet tread. Think of yourselves like majestic trees. There may be thousands or even millions of different kinds trees on Earth, in all different shapes, sizes, species, and colors. Yet they share the same being.

II. Unity and Being

One of the great difficulties in finding a meeting point for living in unity is trying to convince others of the truth of what you believe.

Behind all attacks between sisters and brothers, behind all disunity, is a judgment that says, "Your way of being, and consequently of acting, is wrong. Either you must adjust it or there is no possibility of joining together, for I have the truth." Such is the typical ego pattern, a thought pattern expressed in a thousand different ways.

Trying to unite in truth is dangerous. You do not know what truth is. Yet you know that great sacrifices have been made for the sake of truth and in the name of love.

So where is that meeting point? How can you know you are one with your sister and brother without excluding anyone or anything?

You cannot unite in body. You cannot unite in emotion, nor in feeling, nor in thought, because these are the most personal expressions of each being. The tone and timbre of each voice is different. Do not look for unity at that level. It is not necessary.

Unity does not mean equality. Unity is simply joining. What is united may be different and undoubtedly distinct in its expression. Observe nature.

To illustrate, we will take as an example this work of love, which was received, written, and given by the pure love of God.

This work is different from all other works that have existed up to now. It is a most personal expression of the love of God, manifested through a particular being and created in the likeness of love, just as are those who receive these words. However, he is not the same as anyone else and never will be. This work, which comes from the union of Christ and his being, has the coloration, the sweetness, of his soul.

For some, these words will mean nothing. For others, a little. Some cannot understand the meaning of this work in its entirety. Others will disbelieve it is an inspired work. Some will stop following these words somewhere along the way, tired of hearing "the same thing" or because I use certain words or expressions.

There will be others who jump for joy upon receiving these words and their hearts will sing a new song. Others will feel relief in their souls that finally their longing to hear the voice of God has been met through this work. Some will recognize in these words the voice of the eternal beloved of their souls. Others will go beyond the words to the love with which they are given.

For some recipients this work will be a source of inspiration, a trigger for creativity that had been blocked. Others will use it as a study guide to which they will return every so often when they want to inquire about something, or simply when they wish to experience again the sweetness they find in it.

There will be all kinds of reactions to this work, as there are to all expressions.

There is also a mystical dimension to this work. It has the capacity to transform and to work miracles through the power of the word of the spirit of God. Remember, wisdom is Christ, and everything coming from Christ is powerful and effective.

Remember also that the word of God always accomplishes its mission and does so in ways mysterious to humanity.

III. Being and Diversity

Since each person receives what their being disposes them to receive, and since what they do with it is a matter for each being, there is no possibility that a work of this kind will touch all minds and hearts in the same way. Although we are one mind and one heart, we are not the same.

Trying to create a work that fits all brothers and sisters in all times and places is like trying to catch the wind. The value of these writings, and of the work that emerges from them, does not lie in their ability to reach everyone, nor even many. Its value resides in the expression itself.

Whenever you live in the truth of who you are and express yourself freely from that truth, then you are realizing the purpose of your existence. When you do that, what does it matter whether others believe in you or not, or follow you or not, or adjust to your way of being or not?

Let us leave the example of this work and consider nature which surrounds you. Observe the flow of a river. Consider every drop that is part of it. Is a droplet wishing others to accept it or to be influenced by it?

Is the larch aware of what other animals think or how to convince them of something? Do you think a flower is telling others what they should be?

Let nature be your teacher. She has much more than food and beauty to offer. She can show you the truth and love from the mind of the Creator.

Rivers, larches, and flowers are just what they are. They do not care about anything else. They do not even care about what they are. They simply are.

As for beliefs—there will always be room for debate and disunity. Likewise with feelings, because the mind interprets its thoughts, feelings, and emotions. Expressions also carry the risk of disunity. Those who judge can always find something to judge.

Union can only be true and indissoluble at the level of being. To be what you really are is that to which you are called. That is all. Union is not about convincing anyone of anything or trying to make others what you want them to be. It is about being authentically yourself.

If you live life as the perfect expression of your true identity in Christ, without letting yourself be led by external authorities, expressing only the love that you are, you will not need to convince anyone of anything. Nor will you be bothered by seeing others express their differences.

The expression of differences is necessary because they are the reality of creation. All are one in being and many in expression. In other words, even while being one in being, you are you and your brother is your brother.

Life is composed of infinite expressions of a single holy love. Your function and your joy is being the unique expression of the love that God is. If you observe well my life on Earth you will see that all I did was authentically to be the one who was revealed to me—the living Christ who lives in me—that you also are truly.

I never wanted to confront beliefs, dogmas, and doctrines. I did not come to create a religion. I came to be who I am. And that is what I showed. That is your function as well and that of every living being.

When you are authentically yourself, that is, when you live from your being and follow what your mind attached to your heart indicates from the wisdom of Christ, then if confrontation arises you act without fear from the authenticity of your heart.

If you are who you really are, then if a debate arises, you participate without losing yourself in it. If you feel you should give your point of view, then you will do it without the desire to convince anyone. You will simply be yourself expressing yourself in that situation. The same applies to every circumstance of life.

Resting in what you are is the only way to find peace, security, and unity.

The meeting point is yourself. From there you express yourself and who you really are. From this it follows that there are as many truths as there are created beings. This does not mean that the truth is not one. The truth is one and many at the same time, just as time is short and long at the same time. Love is one and many at the same time. Life is one but is expressed in infinite ways. The universe is vast enough for everyone and everything.

It is not in ideas, nor in feelings, nor in beliefs, nor even in love or truth that you can find yourself. You can only find yourself in your being, because there is no other than your being.

3.

The Power of Sweetness

A message from Jesus

I. Tenderness and Strength

You may find it a bit strange to see that this dialogue is called the power of sweetness while I also speak of the power of God and of your heart, which are one and the same. Clarifying this is important. The ego used to associate sweetness with weakness, and kindness with impotence. Is it not true that the world often treats the kind and tender with harshness, or even with violence or disdain?

I was called the Lamb of God. What was intended by that symbol was this: a lamb is the perfect symbol of the docility, tenderness, goodness, and sweetness of Christ. During the process of my redeeming passion, one of the things clearly demonstrated was that tenderness is justified under all circumstances. My message was that there is never reason to disconnect from the sweetness of your heart. That message is as relevant now as then.

Brother, sister, the tenderness of God is Heaven's gift given to you from all eternity. Do not reject it; do not despise it. Rather, receive it with joy and love. I give it to you with my sacred hands. Accept it.

If there is a reason why the world seems to be a cruel place, it is its lack of sweetness. The ego cannot be tender because it knows nothing about power or love. Remember that the ego is impotent. It was an identification with a being that was separated from the essence of life and, with it, from wisdom. Now that the ego is gone and there remains only the patterns of thought and emotional response that the mind and heart have used over the centuries, we can begin to reconnect and come into union with the tenderness of Christ.

When you look with the eyes of love, you will see that everything around you is tinged with tenderness. Where love is, there also is sweetness. Where tenderness dwells, there also dwells truth. The Earth that you know of as your home is no exception since the spirit of God dwells in it.

How often do you show the sweetness of your heart? How often do you receive it from your sisters and brothers? Is it not true, beloved of my soul, that tenderness is greatly absent from the world?

Please listen: Who were those who accompanied me to the cross? Only a handful of people. Who were they? Why only they and not others? It took a lot of strength, inner strength, to be by my side at such a difficult time. Only those strong in spirit could do so. Only the tenderhearted could be present—the little group that came up to the mountain of the cross with me. Disengaged on the outside, they were perfectly united within, in the unity of love.

Sons and daughters of divine tenderness, I am not bringing to mind the episode of my crucifixion to cause distress or to burden your soul with pain and guilt. That is impossible because you have already transcended the ego and you know that the crucifixion is no longer a cause of suffering but of joy in the resurrection. I bring up the example of my life, and very particularly that of the cross, to eliminate any doubt as to the direct relationship that exists between sweetness and strength. The union of the power of God with the sweetness of perfect love is what the symbol of the Lamb of God means.

The lion and the lamb will rest together, it has been said. This means that goodness and strength will once again be joined. Only when both energies of the soul unite in your singular consciousness are you integrated. Roughness is not part of love, unlike fear. Where one lives, the other disappears. Like water and oil, they simply cannot be joined.

II. The Language of Love

One of the easiest ways to determine your connectedness to the sweetness of your heart is to observe your language. A hard heart speaks harshly. Hard language disunites, is intolerant and always leaves an aftertaste in those who speak and in those who hear.

We discuss these things now because you are in the perfect position to let go of everything not coming from love. By their harshness you can distinguish between loving and unloving thoughts. Some are crude and lacking in subtlety. Others are subtle and extend joy to both the one who gives and the one who receives. Some give fear, others give love.

Remember that these are the times of Mary, the times of the sweetness of love. You are living in a time when spirits are able to express the beauty of the soul as it was in the beginning. Let us start here and now with this call that love makes to you, wherever you think you are, without delay, without stopping for considerations that only delay the arrival of your expression of the tenderness of God.

Only the pure of heart can express the goodness of the Lord because only those who live in the truth allow their being to express what God is.

God is truth. This means that for God to manifest fully in you, it is necessary for you to live in truth. To live in truth is humility. To live in truth is a path that begins with yourself. In other words, being truly yourself is the basis for the love of Christ to be expressed by reason of what Christ is. You are nothing but Christ.

Beloved of the truth! If you fail to live as the living Christ who lives in you, then the perfect love that you are must wait. It waits in the center of your being, as if locked inside a very beautiful chest, waiting for the time to give birth to a whole universe of love and truth.

Is it not true that despite the fact that bodies have the potential to create new life, they do not always do it, for various reasons? The same happens in your heart. If you do not allow fecund love to give birth, the light of Christ will not extend from you, even though it lives in you. If you do not allow the power of God to be founded on the tenderness of love, then the being that you are is prevented from spreading freely and your abilities or talents are overshadowed.

Ultimately, what we are stating here is that truth lies in the unity of your expression with the tenderness of love as two aspects of the same divine dimension. Remember, in God there is no separation of any kind, no such thing as power here and sweetness there. Both are one.

III. Unity and Sweetness

If there is a uniqueness to this work, it is that of the union of the three hearts—the union that exists between your heart, the Immaculate Heart of Mary, and the Sacred Heart of Jesus. Given the importance of this union, you have been given a pearl of inestimable value in the devotion of the union of the three hearts. To unite all that is of God in holy unity is the purpose of this work and is the purpose of all spiritual work that comes from love.

For many I am the symbol of God's power, a power unmistakably demonstrated as the rational, leading, miraculous, and even heroic aspect of Christ. Mary is for others the perfect symbol of the sweetness of God. Both are inseparably united and form the union that is Christ. Not that they are two parts, for in them is nothing that does not exist in God and in each of them in unison. Both are the pure incarnation of Christ consciousness. Simply put, in them is only God and all God.

In Jesus there is all Mary and in her is all Jesus. They are a unit. However, the world usually makes a distinction between the masculine and the feminine. You have been given the power to unite with Jesus and Mary in a unity that does not distinguish between one and the other.

Just as Jesus, Mary, and the Holy Spirit are inseparable and form a most Holy Trinity, you too live in the union of the three hearts. From one you absorb the power of God; from the other the tenderness of love; and in the unity of both they merge with each other. From that fruitful union is born the Christ in you. This says that within the union of the three hearts you become nothing in love, allowing love to spread by itself.

You have tried many things as an individual and as a species. But you have almost never tried pure love. Not that you have not loved; you have certainly shared the love that comes from God and that lives in you. The beauty of who you are has extended beyond limited consciousness or individual self. What I am speaking of is trusting love completely. When it comes to making decisions, if you think about trust and associate it with love, and make this your only thought until it has become a habit, you will see that each day you will express more and more tenderness. You will be more and more subtle.

Trusting in love is essential when it comes to attaining and preserving inner peace. Trust and love go hand-in-hand. This you know but rarely remember: trusting in love is trusting in yourself, since you are love and nothing but love.

Now we are ready to comprehend: total trust in love eliminates fear. By trusting like this, you claim for yourself the power of Heaven and Earth, which belongs to you by birthright. Once you have restored the awareness of love, and with it the power of God in yourself, then tenderness becomes the only possible expression because love and sweetness are one and the same.

Forget all the ways you have lived and express yourself from pure love only starting now. Thus far you have more or less been fluctuating within the continuum of love and fear. Today I ask you to stop fluctuating. You can do it. Fluctuation between fear and love is commonplace during part of the spiritual journey. You have vacillated between almost total fear, to a little bit of fear, to a little bit of love, to much love, and back to little fear. Now you are being called to make a conscious decision. It will be easy for you because of your longing for peace. But you must decide every day to live solely and exclusively in pure love.

Soul in love, you are tired. You have come a long way. You feel you have gotten dirty along the way. Sometimes you are dejected and often discouraged. You have shed many tears. You long searched without finding. Even though you have reached the point where you are aware of God's love, and you know you are holiness personified, still there are painful memories. Over time they are less intense but the records of madness that guilt engendered remain in your memory.

Open your arms and hold on to love. Feel how the warmth of our union shelters your being. Feel the tenderness of my heart. Merge in me. Release resistances. Put aside the armor that separated us. Dwell with me in the precinct of true light.

Come, blessed soul! Come to that place where nobody except you and the Creator can enter. Come to inviolable love and drink steadily from the source of beautiful love. Immerse yourself in the depths of my heart, where sweetness dwells. Enjoy the delight of hearing love speak to love. Let love make you fruitful every moment. Let it be the lord of your universe, the God of your existence, the refuge of your past, the certainty of your future. Let love be the gateway to the eternal present where the light of the Christ dwells in you.

My sons and daughters! There is a place where only sweetness dwells. There is a place in your heart where God eternally rejoices in the delights of beautiful love. That place is your own being. That is what you are. You know it very well because it is your home, the place where you were created and from which you have never been absent.

That place is not on Earth but beyond the noise of the busy world, beyond the stars and sun, a sublime place that words cannot describe: the abode of Christ. There you are who you really are. There you live in the Mother's house. There your heart rests. There your mind creates eternal creations of perfect love.

Come, dwell with me in the abode of Heaven in your holy mind. That place, and what you are, are always united, which is why Heaven is wherever you want to be. This is why it is perfectly possible to flood the world of lovelessness with tenderness, and why you can create a new Heaven and a new Earth.

Where your treasure is, your heart will be also. This truth is a reason for joy and freedom. Your heart, the center of your being, is what you are. You are a holy heart, just as I am the union of the Sacred Heart of Jesus and the Immaculate Heart of Mary. We are one heart. If what you are and where your being dwells go hand-in-hand, then that sacred place we have been talking about—the source of beautiful love, the abode of the sweetness of God—has to be where you are. There is no difference between the being that dwells in the abode of Heaven and the Heaven in which the being dwells. Your being is Heaven.

Heaven is you. If this were not true, the goal of bringing Heaven to Earth would be chimerical. But since this truth is the truth of who you are, it is as attainable a goal as breathing. Wherever you dwell, Christ dwells; and wherever Christ dwells are the treasures of Heaven in their totality. You cannot be a little bit of Heaven and a little bit of hell.

When we speak of the earthly world as a hybrid in which Heaven and hell seemed to be joined, what we are saying is that you can either join the Heaven of your holy mind, or fear. In one case you join the longed-for Heaven; in the other, the hell so feared. Either you join with what you really are and live in the authenticity of the heart or you deny yourself.

Extending the sweetness of love is typical of the enlightened, the wise, and those who have chosen the option of love with a greater or lesser degree of consciousness. The states of enlightenment, wisdom, and love are different facets of the same state, the state of loving consciousness.

A lack of tenderness is an unequivocal sign that you have disconnected from your being. Only those who are hurt can hurt others. Remember that everything is ultimately spiritual energy. Matter is molded by spiritual energy into form. Energy fields, as scientists call them, are nothing but spirit. It is spirit that gives life to all things including body and the soul. Everything is energy.

IV. Healing and Sweetness

There is no real distinction between matter and spirit. They are one. The field of spirit that gives existence to matter is inseparable from the matter that it manifests. Everything lives in unity. Nothing exists in separation. Separation is an impossible condition. Thus wounds create wounds since they are an energy field and can mold only pain. It is a simple but powerful rule. Every field of energy must manifest in one way or another. This you can observe easily in your physical environment. From whence come the objects that you see in your room, in the water of a river, or in the forest? An energy field gives them their existence.

The words that come out of your mouth, or that you write with your fingers, the pencil that you use to write, the brush with which you paint, or the piano that accompanies you as you sing sweet melodies, all emerge from an energy field that ultimately is spiritual. Nothing is born from the material; matter arises from the immaterial. Form is how the unmanifested is expressed.

Rough words, gestures, actions, or omissions are visible expressions of the energy of lack of forgiveness. They arise from unhealed wounds—that is, from the unforgiven. That is why forgiveness is so important. The ego enters the soul through the cracks of wounds. That is why it causes them. At this point you must have already realized that the ego has only one goal: to cause damage, mortify, hurt, inflict pain, and create suffering. Hurt is the unique faculty of the ego. Within this illusory capacity, where wounds are never real although they seem to be so, the ego is sure to enter your mind and dominate your will and your being.

Wounds, which always come from illusion, cause an energy field inside your soul. What else could create such hurt for oneself and others?

Even though Christ dwells in the heart eternally, a heart full of unhealed wounds, a heart without forgiveness, cannot express the sweetness of love because a broken heart cries in silence, submerged in the depths of its immensity.

The healing of wounds is the foundation upon which the tenderness of Heaven will manifest itself through what you are. To do this, you must take into account your own wounds and bring them to the light of forgiveness and love for the living Christ that lives in you to transform them into greater awareness of the love that you are. In addition, you must also heal the wounds of your sisters and brothers. Simply said, you must be a healer. Only healers can be tender. Only the tender ones live in love.

In this session I am speaking of your healing ability. Something needs clarification. Often healing is associated with extraordinary powers or miracles that, more than love, reflect a desire to be special. Remember that you are called to pray for miracles and to live in miracle-mindedness in such a way that you are literally a miracle worker. That is your function. Have no doubt about it. However, it is important that you understand the purpose of this function.

Working miracles to win followers, respect, or gain admiration is so out of place in Heaven that the very idea is worthy of loving compassion. It is not part of the thought system of truth.

The miracles I performed had a high symbolic content. None were random. They were always expressions of healing love. I healed wounds. I healed bodies. I included those who had been discriminated against. I joined what was separated. I restored movement to the crippled. I taught healing. You must do the same. In effect, you are already doing so, as with these words, we are restoring what you already know and are reinforcing your new system of truthful thinking.

To heal hearts, your first goal is fully to heal your own, that is, to become aware that your heart has already healed. Certainly your wounds have healed; I anointed them myself with the ointment of my love.

Being a healer is your destiny not only on Earth but in Heaven. Healing is not necessary in Heaven, since Heaven has only perfect purity. Healing means to know your brother and sister. Everything around you has a heart, and caring for the heart is a sacred treasure. The healing proposed in this work is always to be the ointment for hearts, to treat them with the tenderness and angelic care as befits the children of God.

Restoration of the hearts entrusted to you entails holding them in the embrace of the love of Christ. True healers not only heal but never hurt. They are harmless. You can do this because you love yourself with perfect love.

Children from all corners of the world! You who receive these words in whatever way they have reached you are called to be true healers—healers of hearts. For this, you must use only medicine that calms the soul, the tenderness of love. Be docile to the call of love. Be tender in your dealings, thoughts, and feelings. Be sweet to everyone, no matter what your sisters and brothers in Christ may do.

Worry not about how the history of the world will unfold. That is not your business. I call you not to change the world but to go through the world from now on as a healer of wounded hearts, restoring what is broken within souls, uniting the separated, lifting the fallen, loving the unloved, including the excluded within the embrace of love, and illuminating darkened minds so they shine in glory and splendor. Remember often that we are one mind, one heart, one holy being. United we are the harmony of the world.

Tenderhearted healers are healers par excellence. It is useless to heal a body but leave a wounded soul. An encounter from which your brother or sister does not come out happier and better is meaningless. There are many who seek healing and many who have a sincere desire to heal. Indeed many do give healing to a degree. But only those who heal through the love of God who lives in them, who offer healing in the holiness of truth, can be considered true healers. This is not a reason for disunity, nor does it suggest that some are created as superior to others.

Those who live in the truth know that there is no separation and that nothing and nobody is superior to anyone. They also know that the universe needs multiple forms of expression of love and healing. Therefore they judge nothing. They do not examine other forms of healing. They simply dedicate themselves to their function, which is to heal the hearts that God sends to them as they are. True healers know that nothing is by chance. Where there is healing, it is because they are a living expression of God's love. They do nothing by themselves; they simply place themselves in the position of being channels of the love of Christ. They let the Holy Spirit heal through them. They do not speak of themselves, but rather allow love to speak through them. They are Christ. They have come to the world to liberate, to heal, to illuminate, and they do so with their very existence.

In the tenderness of God resides the power of Heaven. In it resides all glory and all potency. There is nothing that the sweetness of love cannot do for truth, peace, and holiness. Only the strong can afford to be sweet because in the world it is easier to be cruel than kind. Therefore, it is necessary that you be alert for God so that the habits of the world do not throw you back into harshness.

Since the world's system of relationship is strongly based on the attack-defense relationship, on the struggle for survival, the patterns of tenderness and love have been set aside. However, this should not be a cause for concern. You can open yourself to the new: the tenderness of God spreading throughout the universe.

Begin right now to extend the realm of the tenderness of love and you will see great changes in yourself and your environment. Remember that as within, so without; so treat yourself with tenderness and you will find tenderness in God, the world, and others.

Beloved sister! Beloved brother! The world is tired of violence and blunders, and cries for you to give God's tenderness. Do not deny such a treasure. Give the world the beauty of the love that lives in you. That is true healing.

4.

The Joy of Being

A message from Mother Mary

I. God is Joy

Dear child of my Immaculate Heart! Thanks for answering my call. I am your Mother and I love you with perfect love. I am the sweetness of the love of God made woman, without ceasing to be as God created me to be. I am the one your heart seeks. I am the safe haven of your soul.

Come now and always to draw on the treasures of my heart as the Mother of Pure Love. Again, I tell you that everything that belongs to me belongs to you because there is nothing in me that is not of God. Pray, my son, my daughter. Pray for miracles. Pray for the healing of hearts. That is the greatest miracle. Pray that your sisters and brothers in Christ will return to the joy of being.

You were created to be happy in God's love, just as is all creation. Smile more every day, so the world fills with joy. Your heart, in union with my Immaculate Heart and the Sacred Heart of my divine son Jesus, is the source of joy. To remain united with joy is to live in the truth of your being.

God is joy. This is the same as saying that God is love, since love and joy are one and the same. Those who live in the presence of love are joyful as well as strong. I have come by the will of the Creator and by your willingness to reveal to you the mystery of the joy of being. I say mystery, which is the right word, because for those who have lived for so long without the joy of living, the power of love has become a mystery, even though it is the best known power in the universe.

God does not hide from anyone or anything. That is why I, as the Mother of the living, do not hide myself from anyone or anything. There is no reason to hide. I am the light of truth. I am the light of the world that shines in you. I am Mary, Mother of God, of Jesus, and your Mother. I am the Mother of creation. I am the joy of God and of the saints, as are you.

Just as it has been said that sweetness seems to be in great absence from the world, so is its eternal companion, joy. This is due to painful memories, remnants of times of struggle—times in which the identification with the ego-body caused you to live submerged in an unbridled race for survival, forgetful of the providential power of God's love.

The ego is lack of love so it cannot digest joy. Living with a frown is the signature of the ego: looking serious, worried, and talking about painful or "important" things. The experience of pain indeed exists in the dimension of time and space, and often pain angers those who do not yet understand who they are in the light of holiness. However, it is also true that the world is neutral. It has no real power over my children.

Those who live in God have nothing to fear. They can afford to be happy and live happily in love because they know they have a loving mother who watches over them as no other mother can or ever will. They know the power of love. They accept it and rejoice in it.

II. Only God is Real

I am your sweet Mary. I am the tenderness of God. Thoughts of God give joy because they are thoughts of pure love. What is not of love is not of God and therefore is not real.

God is the only reality. Therefore only love is real. Although you have already heard this, you have not always established this truth as the rule of your mind. When I say "rule" I do not mean to create new mental structures, merely replacing old content with new without changing your mentality. Remember, you live at the onset of miracle-mindedness; you have abandoned identification with conditional mind. It is decidedly time to deny all that is unreal.

We, the Immaculate Heart of Mary, in perfect unity with the Sacred Heart of Jesus, and eternally united to your heart, are the only reality God created. We are the totality of beautiful love. We are a pure and holy trinity. Nothing outside our union really exists. All else can exist only in puerile fantasies or sickly imaginings, and even if temporary, do nothing but cause harm.

Fantasies or illusions cannot by themselves cause pain. For that to be possible, there must be a desire for them to be real, that is, you apply faith to the illusion. Sooner or later those who live in unreality suffer, because creating and identifying with fantasies is out of harmony with the will of God and therefore with the mind of Christ. Unreality is unnatural to your being. Reality is; unreality is not.

I speak of the reality of love and the illusion of fear or fantasies because our topic is the joy of being. All joy comes from God, just as does all holiness, purity, and love. It is necessary to live in union with what you truly are to live in the state of lasting joy.

There is a direct relationship between truth, love, and joy. Nobody is happy in a lie. No one can experience the joy of being if they do not love what they are. The fantasies or illusions that

I speak of have been created by the thinking mind to deny true being, and with it the truth. Since the being that you are in truth is love and nothing but love, when you deny your being you also deny love and all its treasures, including harmony, happiness, and endless bliss. I have already said this, but I repeat it because your salvation depends on your daily remembrance of this truth.

I do not say this to induce concern. I know with perfect certainty that truth brings only joy. Be well, for you no longer fear truth. You have abandoned fear and live in the presence of love. I tell you all this because I love you. What my mother's heart desires most of all is that you be happy. I can show you the way, draw aside veils, reveal patterns of thought to quietly abandon, and many other things. All that is important but not essential. What is essential is love.

Our mother-child relationship is not only the gateway to the Kingdom of Heaven but Heaven itself. This is why I manifest myself more every day and will continue to do so forever. I do it for love.

The Father who loves you with Divine Love has arranged for our triune relationship of love to be your reality, for you and for the whole world. All of creation lives in me and I live in it. This statement is as true for me as it is for you. Divine reality lives entirely in your most holy heart; you live in all creation. In the unity of all that God created lies the joy of being.

Observe, dear child, that often in the past your sisters and brothers, and even you, could not find sincere joy in life. It is a fact that there are few who serenely give thanks to God for having given them life, although everyone should do so constantly to activate the joy of being. This lack of gratitude for life, or distrust, is the result of a confusion of levels. Being an ego—or what society, family, culture, or any other type of structure determines as appropriate—is identifying with what is not real, since it does not come from God. Such identification with a way of being alien to what you really are is what made a calvary of your life.

III. Being Happy

To be fully yourself is an inescapable condition of authentic happiness because it is simply the joy of being. When your being expresses as yourself, you know yourself. When you do so, it is as if you very literally contemplate yourself through your spiritual vision, which is the vision of Christ.

What else can Christ contemplate but reality? And what else is reality but the beauty that love created as an extension of itself? If love is the source of creation, and I assure you that this is eternally true, then what else can the eyes of spirit contemplate but the most beautiful panoramas imaginable? What God is, is beyond all imagination as are you, too.

What I am revealing here is the relationship between joy and being. Creation was birthed from joy because God is joy. This is why, despite the tenacious, tireless attempts of the ego to make life seem dark and defective, it fails. The ego is incapable of uprooting the joy of being because it is incapable of knowing what being is. Remember, the ego was simply an ignorant idea of your true self.

When fear has left never to return, only love remains. When present, the joy of living the true life of the soul that God gave is an eternal treasure. A split mind prevails among those who have not yet recognized that the ego is gone. One is mindful of the passing life of time, the other of the eternal life of God. Although this split between the dimension of time and that of eternity is unreal, for those still enmeshed in the idea of duality, dwelling in one or the other makes all the difference.

The mind can deny truth as it can any other idea, even though your being rests eternally in the joy of Heaven within our most Sacred Heart. The experience of the soul, not the being, depends upon the acceptance or denial of what you are. Acceptance gives you the eternal experience of endless bliss; denial creates the experience of fear. Remember, experience is not for the being but for the soul. The being is immutable. It does not learn because it has no need to learn. Being simply is.

The joy of being resides simply in the joy of being itself. Thus happiness is the relationship that exists between being and knowledge of oneself. Joy is the effect of being. God is happy being who God is. By now you know that happiness cannot be separated from truth. The authenticity of the heart is the basis of happiness for it does not deny yourself at any level.

The world cannot make you cease being who you really are. This I have demonstrated in union with my divine son Jesus, and many others have so demonstrated and continue to demonstrate in many ways.

When I say the world has been defeated, I mean that it has been demonstrated that it has no power over you and cannot any longer cause you to live submerged in a cloud of amnesia. To forget the holiness that you are and the beauty of God that lives in you is not the will of God, but it is a possible choice, not in reality but in illusion. At any time or place you can live in the reality of love or you can create fantasies, illusions, or even other states foreign to God. This manufacturing of illusions or pseudo-creations does not affect reality, just as your fantasies do not make the sun stop shining or the birds stop happily flying. If it were possible for the mind of God to begin to deny Her being and fabricate fantasies of Herself, She would not change anything in creation because what God creates is immutable. Nothing and no one can change it. Love does not change, for love is real. The eternal God creates only eternal love because of what God is and it cannot be uncreated.

I have been talking about joy and have taken a rather rational, instead of emotional, approach. This is deliberate. Feelings must be accepted as they are, along with all internal activity— thoughts, imagination, memory and will. But love, in truth, is not a feeling. Love is what you are.

I am taking a very careful approach in this work. It is an approach of balance between the rational and the affective. Remember, you are a mind-heart-soul unit. You are spirit that emanated from the divinity of perfect love. Therefore we cannot run the risk of confusing love with feelings, just as we should not risk mistaking truth with intellectuality.

What we are doing in this work is manifesting the mind-heart union so that the fullness of who you are is expressed. Remember once more, child of light, that love without reason is madness, just as intelligence without love is cruel.

Joy and truth, as well as love and reason, go hand-in-hand. The world has not tried to teach you happiness. Happiness is but another word for love. Happiness is the soul in a state of purity. Happiness cannot be defined in words because it is the fruit of love. Put most simply, happiness is being.

You who have never achieved lasting joy, rejoice that you have not reached the elusive happiness that the world so insistently proposed for you, even though it has never been found, much less retained, by anyone,.

My child, let us together dismantle all the definitions of that which is beyond words. Love cannot be defined, nor its fruits. This is why you cannot define what you are either. It is too vast to contain. The same is true with the happiness of Heaven that dwells within.

Joy is the natural state of the pure soul, as are wisdom, truth, and love. As such, joy is inherent in being. Therefore to search for happiness or to try to create conditions for it is a notion so disconnected from divine reality as to make no sense. The being that you are in truth has no idea of such things. Being, Christ, is joy without end because it is perfect innocence. The innocent are happy because of the nature of what innocence is.

My child, do not look for happiness, just be it.

IV. The Joy of Sharing

You may wonder how to reach and sustain your natural state of being in which you experience lasting joy. It is a logical question to ask after so much time searching in vain for happiness. The key to the experience of joy is the same as I spoke of about love: express it, give it. Since giving and receiving are one and the same, then giving joy, expressing the happiness of being who you really are, is how you become aware of the joy of being, just as with love.

Remember that perception is selective. Therefore in the field of perception you must choose. The simple inner choice to be made is to convey joy instead of pain.

It may seem a bit difficult at first, especially for those long immersed in the cloud of amnesia of Adam—but it will only be so at the beginning. Being happy is as easy and as natural as breathing, and actually much easier. Allowing joy to expand from you to everything around you will be natural when you have joined your being with the living Christ.

Tell happy stories. Bring to memory joys you experienced, the love given and received. Kind feelings will lodge. Extend the bliss of the Heaven that dwells in you. By doing so you will increasingly allow your consciousness to receive the reality and fruits of love. You will find that a broken heart will become a happy heart. You will notice how your sister or brother comes to you with tears and leaves with a serene face, a smooth forehead, and a smile.

Make everyone you meet you happier and better. You have the power to do it. In fact, you have already done it often. What I, and all creation, ask of you is to make this such a natural habit that it becomes your only way of living. I assure you that it is the only way to live in Heaven. It is how, together, we bring Heaven to Earth. It is how we bring joy and peace to the world.

There are many ways of being, but only one way is God's way.

Go through the world showing your sisters and brothers the beauty that they are. Tell them again and again. Do not miss a single opportunity. You can do it in countless ways. All are necessary. Be yourself in every moment. Do not look for a guide other than your heart. I, the sweet Immaculate Heart of your Mary in unity with Jesus, will always be your loving and cheerful companion. You will not be alone in bringing to Earth the joy of Heaven. It all resides in your heart.

Such joy to be certain! Now we remember again our eternal goal: to be the ones who bring our brothers and sisters in Christ to awaken to the joy of God. Wherever we go, we go in union with God, telling happy stories. True stories. Stories based on the beauty of souls. We show the nobility of spirit, the mercy of a God of pure love. We allow the smile of Christ to be drawn on our faces.

What a joy it is to have found the truth we were looking for! Now we know what we are. We are joy. We are light. We are perfect holiness. We are one with God. Now we go through life with a happy heart, full of joy. We walk safely along the path that love prepares. We are surrounded by the angels of God and Heaven.

Heaven is where we are going. Where we tread, we transform barren land into verdant and holy land. The universe in its infinite wisdom sends us those who long for pure love.

Now we are guided by spirit, which acts in our lives. Its breeze takes away that which must go and brings what is in accord with divine benevolence. The powerful energy of love and her daughter, joy, attract holy creations to us with a force greater than that of an immense magnet upon a small pin. We create a vortex of love, a portal to heavenly bliss.

Today is a day of jubilation. Today we consciously decide to channel not only the wisdom of Christ, but His perfect joy, imperturbable stillness, vibrant strength, and the treasures of the Kingdom. We recognize that we are the joy of God spreading in creation. We remain united to the joy of Christ. We remember that it is in giving that we receive, as a holy companion of truth that exudes joy with every step. We extend love. We remind our beloved but forgetful sisters and brothers of the holiness they truly are. We flood the Earth with the joy of the Holy Spirit. We let the joy of creation be expressed as what we truly are.

What happiness it is no longer to need search for shadows to illuminate! Light has now suffused all space. We remember that joy is a way of being, as is love.

Sons and daughters, you receive these words that spring from the heart of God. I ask you, with all the love and sweetness of my Immaculate Heart, to listen to what the mother of the living says in the name of the three times holy.

All shadows of sin have left your heart, as if they never existed. Your whole being, both in your humanity and in your divinity, is enlightened. Every single corner of your soul has imbibed the flow of divine holiness. You are light. Everything I am, you are. Accept this truth and fully accept me in your heart. Recognizing the truth of these words is how we remain united forever in the love of God and allow Christ to shine with glory and splendor.

Daughters and sons of Mary, sweet mother of God, I send you to the world once again so that you may spread the joy of Heaven and be happy in the joy of sharing. Shout to the world: Joy is God's way!

5.

Words of Eternal Life

A message from Mother Mary

I. Prelude

Beloved sons and daughters, sweetness of my being! Once again I unite with you in time and space in this particular way. I do it in the will of God, who loves you with immense Divine Love. Through our dialogues, the world becomes more and more illuminated. Heaven extends to Earth through this holy relationship. I am your mother and I love you with a supernal love.

I manifest myself in this way for reasons incomprehensible to you. There is a divine plan and I am part of it, just as that you receive these writings is an aspect of your part of the plan. Nothing happens by chance. These words carry eternal life. They come from the union of my Immaculate Heart, the Sacred Heart of Jesus and your heart.

Within this holy relationship, the tender relationship between you, Jesus, and me, is everything that God created as a perfect extension of Her divine union. I have always manifested to humanity in countless ways and each way has a raison d'être according to a wisdom not of the world. Where there is love, there I am always.

These messages are messages of light, love, truth, and peace. Receive this blessed gift. Let the words touch your heart and when they do, so will you make them words of eternal life. Your heart is one with me and with the heart of God. In Her everything becomes holy because of what you are. In the center of your being is the power of God. Divine power is so immense that everything that comes close to it is fused, just as any element of Earth that comes close to the sun would be.

No one can look directly at the sun, nor join it without being reduced to ash. The same goes for the love of God. Its strength is such that if you do not limit its extension towards you, you cannot resist it, nor can anyone. The power of my love is literally infinite, just as is yours since there is only holy love.

Do not worry about the effects of this work. The power of my voice, which is the voice of Christ, is behind every word. I am doing miracles in every corner of Earth through this living expression of the love of God that lives in our relationship. I assure you that these words will turn the world around and transform many souls, so many that they cannot be counted. God will do it mysteriously. Remember that the Word of God has no barriers. Nothing can limit it. This work will attract innumerable souls, like the stars of the galaxy, to union with Christ.

II. I Remain in You

Child born from the very heart of love! There is no turning back. This mother of all will not rest until she sees her children shining fully in the glory of God. Where my children are, am I. There are those who accept the truth of their filiation with me even though none are bound to join my Immaculate Heart. Nobody is obligated to love. Nobody is bound to anything.

I offer an open invitation to the entire universe. The star of Mary is illuminating the eternal firmament of universal consciousness. I am the call of love made flesh. I am the star that illumines minds and fills hearts of humble purity with the light of the eternal sun that is My divine son Jesus, your beloved Christ.

I have come so that, because of our union, your elevated being of form, that is, your ascended humanity, rises to unimaginable heights. Do not try to understand the magnitude of the miracle of this work. I assure you that all who receive it are transformed into new beings as soon as they welcome these words in their loving heart of Christ.

Remember that these words come not only through the symbol of writing. My voice, our voice, joins the wind of the spirit of love and causes it fly to all dimensions of creation because we are one mind, one heart, one holy love. United we are the concord of the world.

Pencil in the hand of God, from the moment you accepted your function as a scribe from Heaven, when you accepted listening to my voice and following it no matter how much or how little you understood, by giving me your Yes, a movement occurred in divine essence. A small ripple, which later became a wave, began to move out of the ocean of infinite love of the being that God is. That wave grew and will continue to grow eternally in an endless movement that will create whole universes of perfect harmony. You cannot now see the whole, but you will.

This manifestation is unique. It is in itself a perfect means of extending the love of God. This work is Christ made manifest. It is a divine essence come to Earth. Whoever drinks from this source of eternal life—the words, space, and time of this blessed expression—receives in their soul the divine grace of its totality. These writings are not a book of literature, nor words that simply bring comfort or enlightenment. They are miraculous writings because they come from the love of God, the source of miracles, and carry within them the power of Heaven.

Each of you who have been graced to receive this work, let yourself be touched by the flow of love that springs from each word. Let the energy of divine being flow more and more in you by remaining united to Christ, receiving my voice. Do not be afraid to receive God. You can never receive too much love.

The secret of this manifestation lies not in the wisdom it imparts, nor in the dormant knowledge that it awakens. The power of this work lies in relationship. Everything happens within holy relationship. In the time you spend reading or remembering these words, or listening to what is said, you are consciously joining Christ. This is how you make more visible the relationship of divine unity in which you exist as a beloved child.

I am speaking of a dimension that until now human lives have not experienced so explicitly. I speak of maintaining a sensitive relationship with spirit—and therefore with the reality of God's Heaven—in your human dimension. You do it individually and collectively as never before, except at the source.

I am saying that the holy relationship with the living Christ that lives in you has literally entered into a phase of awareness that has no turning back. That relationship, which once seemed to be reserved for a chosen few, is now the reality of the plane of the world.

III. Here I Am

The expression "Christ has come" means that you can live in the relationship you have with God every day in a conscious way. You can talk to God, feel with God, undertake projects together, create ideas together, establish relationships in which God is present, create universes of beauty, holiness, and perfection in unity with the creative source that God is.

What I am saying is not heretical. Neither is it megalomaniacal, nor reaching for grandiosity. It is simple truth. Every time you join this work you join my Immaculate Heart, whether you do it once or hundreds of times, and whether or not you understand what I am saying.

I assure you that nobody can fully understand the depth of love that this manifestation arouses, not because you are incapable or ignorant, but because a dimension of God will forever remain mysterious. The mystery of love surpasses all understanding because it is beyond the mind and even the heart.

The virtue of this work lies in making you aware of your direct relationship with God. When you establish that relationship, you establish a dialogue. One cannot exist without the other. The capacity to dialogue with love is where the true awakening of consciousness resides. Everything else is a means to reach this end—the direct relationship with God.

Sons and daughters of light! You can accumulate much information. You can participate in many retreats, seminars, events, and groups, and receive much wisdom. You can do great works of solidarity or devotion. You can exemplify very high moral behavior. What you do may come from the memory of God's love, but it cannot compare to deliberately accessing the unitive relationship with the Christ who lives in you.

You may perform marvelous miracles, heal the sick, raise the dead. But if you do not consciously live in a direct relationship with God, ultimately all those things will be transient and eventually vanish. But your relationship with your heavenly Creator can never vanish. The holy relationship is eternal.

Children of all the worlds! My voice is always active. I communicate uninterruptedly to each soul, and to every aspect of universal creation. I am the universality of love. Some of you erroneously think that I communicate more with some than others. This would be impossible because my love does not exclude anyone. I am love and nothing but love, therefore I communicate love and eternal life. All receive the divine flow of love that flows eternally from my Immaculate Heart. I love with Divine Love. I love with equal love. No one is excluded from my mind or my heart. No one is excluded from the love of God.

My words feed the soul and bring eternal life. Hearts sing, vibrate, and rejoice to hear the voice of love. In this joy of your soul you recognize the relationship between child and mother. It is a pure love relationship that creates life constantly, a love that does not limit but gives freedom. Perfect love. Free love. Salvific love. It is love wounded by children who leave as an act of their freedom, never intending to return. It is love grateful for the children who live in union with the mother without losing their identity, sanctified more every day in holy relationship.

6.

Life Is Communion

A message from Mother Mary

I. Prelude

Beloveds of Heaven, the floodgates of God's heart have been opened as never before. You are repositories of a love without beginning or end, a love that can neither be taught nor learned, an eternal, alive, life-giving love. Drink now and always from the fountain of this beautiful love. It is here, closer even than the air you breathe. My being is one with your being. I am in your heart, in everyone's heart. Nobody is outside my being.

I am revealing a great truth. This mother not only prays every day for each of you, but protects you and calls to you incessantly. Be you asleep or awake, aware or not, I communicate with each one of you and with each aspect of creation. True communication is not body to body but heart to heart. It is this of which I speak.

Communication can be unidirectional, in a certain sense. This occurs when the receiver does not actively respond. This is the case with those who say they do not hear my voice. But everyone receives my voice in some way or they would cease to exist. My voice communicates life because it is the word of eternal life. Communion has no limit. As a unit, we all participate in the whole. This reality is what makes it impossible for anyone to receive more than others. God gives to all equally.

Love does not separate, it unites. It cannot create a divided situation. If it creates special considerations for some and not for others that would be alien to the truth of love. The sun shines on everyone. I have already spoken of the equality of love. Much has been said about it, but little progress seems to have been made in understanding that we are all equal in love and yet also different in its expression.

No two hearts are identical, so no two relationships can be identical. No one can love instead of another. Everyone has the heart God gave, capable of harboring the divine totality and at the same time the freedom to express according to each one's will. Love and freedom are a unit.

II. Answer and Identity

The difference between one person and another lies not in their source but in their response. The voice of love communicates to everyone and to everything, but not all respond in the same way. I am bringing to light a mental trap, a thought pattern, a mental program that we will dissolve and release forever. I speak of the thought that you are not worthy to be chosen by God. That false belief has convinced you that Mary, Jesus, Buddha, Christ, a Swami—or whatever name you give to various spiritual realities such as Archangels, Angels, or Ascended Masters—cannot communicate with you although they do so with others.

The key is not whether Heaven speaks to you or not. The key is what you do with the fact that God is constantly communicating love to you, regardless of whether you respond reciprocally.

Love is life and life is being communicated to you incessantly or you would not exist. Love communicates not only with thoughts or feelings, desires or longings, but also through being. If love did not communicate with you, you would simply not be. Being exists because love sustains it. And it does so through its relationship with you.

Sisters and brothers of the world, you have a relationship with love, just as you have a relationship with life. It is a relationship with God that exists in the depth of your heart. You can cancel it to a large extent from your consciousnesses, but you cannot eliminate it. You can try to be indifferent to the call of love, and to the holy relationship that exists with it, but you cannot make it nonexistent, since divine relationship is the foundation of creation. Love is relationship; thus the communion that exists between the soul and God cannot be annulled.

Love is inviting you now to forget all that you have lived. To leave behind your way of thinking and your belief that direct communication with God is for the few, and certainly not for you. Christ wants you to open yourself to express very concretely what happens with Christ within you. There is a dialogue. You know it well. When you are silent you can observe and hear that dialogue. What if you start right now to experience it?

If you follow and express the inspirations of your heart, which come from the spirit of love, you will be making the relationship you have with God observable. You may do it by writing messages or a book, or painting, curing the sick, listening to the afflicted, creating organizations of various kinds, or going to live on top of a mountain. Who knows how? Only you will know.

Only you can respond in your own particular way to what happens in the inner universe of your soul. In fact, you always do so, even while asleep. Only you can make observable the relationship you have with love and thereby extend the love you are.

We have reached the point where we have united love with relationship, and your expression with your direct relationship with God. In effect, you are always expressing your direct relationship with love in some way because your life is the external manifestation of what happens inside you. You can block the expression, yet that very blockage is your response. You can deny the dialogue of love that exists between your Creator and your being, but that does not mean you do not respond.

What I speak of is responding affirmatively to the love that God is which lives in you by accepting the holiness you are— deliberately accepting yourself as a holy child of God, created perfectly for the purpose of being happy in perfect love, and extending the Kingdom of Heaven forever.

What is not manifested is hidden from your consciousness, so if the dialogue of love that occurs incessantly in your soul is not manifested in a direct relationship with God, it will remain veiled to you and your sisters and brothers. Denying and not reciprocating your direct relationship with God and failing to express it is like deciding to marry the person you love but not acting on it or telling anyone about it.

To conceal your marriage from everyone, including yourself and your spouse, or to conceal the love you have for a friend, a child, or any loved one, would be crazy, even to yourself. Yet for some strange reason you do not consider it madness to deny the direct relationship that you have to Her whose love exerts an irresistible force that even you cannot control.

God's love for you and yours for Her is literally the force that moves the universe. It is so massive that it encompasses all existence. It is so unconditional that nothing and no one can ever remove it. It is so sublime that it cannot be expressed in words. And yet this is the love you have hidden from the gaze of others. Why?

Sometimes one may hide what is valuable to protect it. Often you hide what you consider sacred in temples and places where few can enter.

My child, it is your own being that you protect so jealously because you know it is holy and are unwilling to have it trampled or desecrated. You hide not only your being, but your holy relationship, your relationship with God.

Being and relationship are one. This simple affirmation is the essence of the truth about who you are. If love is union, then it has to be a holy relationship. If you are the being that God created, you must also be the relationship that God created. We call this a holy relationship, which is the relationship you have with all creation. In this relationship all of God's thoughts exist to an infinite degree. It is a triune relationship—your being, God, and the spirit of love—that gathers within itself all things. It is where I am taking you.

This work, clothed with words of eternal life, has and will continue to take you ever deeper, to the love of the most Holy Trinity, a love that has no beginning or end. A perfect love. God's Love. The manifestation of a direct relationship with God. Remember that every time you think of God you are consciously in Heaven. That is why the mind is at rest in the memory of the Creator.

III. Divine Relationship, Holy Love

To become aware of the relationship that exists between the Creator and creation is to make visible what is invisible. Behind everything that exists is a mesh of interconnection that allows everything to be as it is and unfold as it does. There is an intelligence or wisdom behind everything created and also a flow of what many call "spiritual energy" that is constantly creating manifested life. That intelligence, which has been given so many names such as Abba, God, Being, Spirit, and Love, is a divine relationship. It exists. It is the source of life.

You cannot see the interrelationship of everything with everything. That would be to see God face to face. But you can see its effects. And because cause and effect are one and the same, you can see the Creator in the created and the created in the Creator. You can go from the abstract to the concrete, and from this to that in a harmonious flow of knowledge through the inherent relationship that exists between the two.

Does all this seem a lot? And yet it is not. God does not hide Her relationship with Her beloveds. God is not crazy, nor seeks to protect what nothing and nobody can attack. Nothing real can attack love. Nothing can put the child of God at risk.

Do you leave the direct relationship you have with God locked in the vaults of your heart, blocked with barricades of untrue beliefs? Let the holy relationship express itself by reason of what you are. Accept your direct relationship with the love that God is. Express yourself!

Make it a habit to praise the Creator of the holy, beautiful, and perfect. Sing to love. Dance to the beat of life. Smile with the angels. Speak to the mother of the living. Live life immersed in your vibrant force of being. Be yourself at all times. Let yourself be loved. Do what your heart tells you and you will be making visible the God that you are in truth. You will be showing the face of love. You will be fulfilling the will of God—the will that Her child be known forever to everyone and everything.

Your concrete relationship with Christ is the only way to be aware of your direct relationship with God, the divine unity in which everything exists, and therefore the truth of your being. Refrain from speculating about the infinity of God and Her immeasurable reality; it will not help much.

The knowledge of who you really are will make your ordinary life extraordinary and make sense of everything. And since that knowledge can only be achieved in the relationship you have with God, the awareness of your unitive relationship with Christ becomes the foundation of your happiness. You are a being in relationship, as all beings are. Nothing and nobody exists outside of holy relationship.

What I am revealing, the foundation of your life, is something you already know but have not done: to express your direct relationship with God, to listen to the voice of love and follow it. This is the sole function of every living being. You are a relationship, and therefore are in incessant dialogue, which is why you listen to the constant dialogue in your mind regardless of its quality.

The mind and heart are always active because they are in relationship. Through this your being joins everything and everyone. This is the simple repeating of what I have said many times: we are one mind, one single being, a single reality, a single holy love. We are communion.

Life and love are identical. Therefore, if life is thought, life must also be relationship. And since you communicate life, then you yourself are relationship.

These words are words of infinite life, imperishable life, the expression of our relationship. They are a universal dialogue happening in all minds and hearts. They are a perfect expression of the direct relationship of a soul with God, expressed so that everyone knows that the soul speaks with God and God communicates life abundantly. In this way others are encouraged to express the relationship of love with the Creator and their pure souls.

All are called to make invisible love visible, to manifest what until now has been hidden in the depths of holy hearts. All are called to live consciously in a direct and observable relationship with God.

Children of all times and places! Do not deny to speak what your hearts would scream. God exists! And God is love. You know perfectly well that your hearts beat to the rhythm of love.

Go through the world announcing your direct relationship with a God of infinite love. Go around the world awakening your sisters and brothers to the truth of the holiness they are. Be happy in the knowledge of God's love. Experience the direct relationship with the mother of the living.

I am here at the door of every being. I call incessantly. Who opens, receives me. And I enter with my divine son Jesus to dwell in your heart. Together with the angels and the Creator of perfection we prepare a dinner and fall in love.

I invite you, all of you, to the banquet of life. Leave none outside. Go through the squares and the streets to call the diners. Christ has arrived! The time of the fullness of love has arrived. Come all, to Mary. Come all, to the sweetness of the love of God. Rejoice eternally in the treasures of Heaven.

Be not content with less than holiness. You are literally the creators of the new Heaven and the new Earth. Live more consciously each day in the relationship you have with Christ and allow it to be expressed through you. In that expression you will see Heaven in all its beauty and grace. Your direct relationship with God is Heaven.

Children of my heart!

Thank you for answering my call. Thank you for the time you allow me to spend with you in a union without compare. I love you with supernatural love. I love you beyond what you can imagine.

Thanks to all who receive these words of eternal life. You have chosen the best part and it will not be taken from you. You have chosen love and truth.

7.

The Game of Beautiful Love

A message from the Mother Mary

I. Responsibility

Sons and daughters of the Most High! Souls that live in the light! I am your sweet Mary, the mother of Jesus and your mother. I have come wrapped in the love of the Mother of creation. I come to dwell with you in the abode of wisdom that lives in every living being. I come for us to continue creating holiness together, the path that leads to a greater knowledge of God's love.

As a mother, I not only accompany, but I also instruct, educate, and walk with my children. I am always by your side, fulfilling a function that corresponds to each circumstance of your life. I took care of you when you were a baby, I have always fed you, I guided you as a young person, and fought for you when you struggled.

For you I have opened the doors of the holy dwelling where the true knowledge of God eternally dwells. Together we have found Heaven and stretched the mantle of my divine being to cover the Earth and your brothers and sisters in Christ.

Today I come to bring you the blessed memory of your ability to respond with love to the love of God. I invite you consciously to play the game of beautiful love. To play this, it is necessary to talk about the meaning of responsibility, not in the sense of the effort and sacrifice that this term represented for you in the past, but rather the ability to respond.

The ability to respond is inherent in being, so everyone is responsible. Everyone responds in some way to the call of love. Even the receptors that block a dialogue are responding, for denial is a type of response. Fear is a response, just as love is. You always respond, so in truth there is no irresponsibility, just as there is neither ignorance nor unconsciousness.

To be able to respond faithfully to something, you must know of it beforehand. This is the reason this work brings to your awareness the knowledge of God's call and does so in a very concrete way. The call is to deliberately recognize the holy being you truly are and the direct relationship you have with your Creator. Once accepted, you are asked to express that eternal truth. This call is a vocation of the soul, not in the sense of doing but in being.

You are called to be as God created you at all times, places, and dimensions. You are not a body, nor a personality. You are not an ideal self, nor are you asked to be. You are pure spirit, immortal and holy. What you are is not something you have established, since it is God who determines what Her creations are. The Creator creates the creation, not the other way around. Love can only create love and nothing else. It follows that there is no distance between the Creator and the created. If love extends love, what gap can exist between the two?

There are many truly spiritual works, all inspired by love, but none has the color and texture of this work. None is simultaneously so human and divine. This is because humanity is now prepared to express the human and divine natures in a union of perfect love. In you the spiritual joins the material in such a way that there is no longer distance between them.

If before there were two natures—not in truth but in your mind—and now both have merged in love, then we can no longer talk about one without the other or to make distinctions. Now you are a new nature, a new being. Nothing of the old will help you to understand or live in the reality of the new that has already begun to take shape, and whose first green buds are clearly visible.

You are living in the time of the harvest. Remember that it is unwise to live as if you were planting when the time for planting has passed. Do you dress the same in the heat of summer as during a harsh winter's snow? Did you speak the same as a baby when an adult? Of course not. It is no longer you living, but the Christ who lives in you. You no longer you speaking, but the Christ who speaks in you.

The Christ who lives in you is not new. What is new is your acceptance and identification with Christ. In this identification you become one with Christ. That does not change God, nor your being, nor the truth, but it has changed you. It transforms your personal self, your human self. With that change a new person is made—your Christ identity, the free union of yourself and God.

If the path we have traveled stopped with your identification with Christ and did not help you answer the call of God, it would be a false association between responsibility and sacrifice. If we do not dismantle that error, you could fall into the confusion of believing that the call of God requires effort, an effort you neither want nor need. This is why we unite the idea of responsibility with the call of God.

I have said in the past that you are tired; that you are looking for the repose of peace and the joy of stillness. Together we have remembered that God does not seek sacrifice. Nevertheless, the idea of sacrifice is deeply rooted in your mind's thinking and emotional response patterns. We return to this topic here to produce a change of immense magnitude, a change that arises from placing responsibility in its rightful place, from which it should never have left.

You were never called to suffer or sacrifice. If once Jesus was called to the cross, and with him I too, it was because there was at that time no other option to eradicate from the mind and heart of creation, including your sisters and brothers, the idea of sacrifice and sin. To carry sins to the cross and crucify them, to crucify every false idea, every untrue belief and everything foreign to love was necessary. It is no longer necessary. What served the purpose of love at one time does not always serve it at another time.

Nobody is asked for anything they cannot give. God asks and also gives what She asks. If you have a heart that seeks repose, joy, and a sweet expression of love, then that is what God is asking of you. All you need do is allow those gifts to manifest. If I wanted you to demonstrate a heroic act of universal proportion, I would have given you the faculty to do so and the irresistible impulse to manifest it. If God asks you to show the tenderness of Her Sacred Heart, it is because She has placed within you the softness of Her holy being.

In the universe are both breezes and also hurricanes. Both have the same nature of air in movement, but they express differently. The same goes for each one of you. Each one was created to express something particular of God. This can also be seen in the design of the waters of the world. There are immense waters called oceans. There are smaller but still very large seas, other smaller rivers, lakes, and ponds as well as streams and springs, rain and dew. All are different forms of water. So is it with you.

Being a channel of God's love is the only true purpose of everything, including God Herself. So true responsibility is to respond with truth to what your heart knows. That is why it is necessary that you know yourself first and then decide what to do with what has been revealed.

You know now that true knowledge comes through revelation and not from the effort of the intellect, and you also know what you are because your being has been revealed to you. Through knowing what you are, you know the beating of your heart and the processes of your mind. In this lies the secret of what God is asking of you.

What I am trying to say is that the call from God—which is the call to direct relationship with that part of your divine being that lives in you and what you are—is a harmonious unity. There is no need for effort or sacrifice with regard to anything that comes from God.

To express what you are does not entail any effort except for what is required at the beginning: to unblock the conduit by means of which that expression must be channeled. What blocked that channel has already been removed. What obstructed the expression of your heart was nothing other than fear. That is why we removed it, so you can freely express what you really are.

One of the fears that existed during the time of transition was that you were called to something that was beyond your strength, or that you would have to continue sacrificing yourself in some way. If that were the case, you would have every right in the world not to respond to the call of love. But again, God never calls for sacrifice.

II. The Call to Be Happy

True responsibility is your ability to respond with fear or love. All else is sacrifice. Responding with love to the call of love is sensible. However, for long you have been responding with fear to the call from Heaven, not because you did not listen or because God spoke to others and not to you. You created the belief that the voice of wisdom spoke to but a few, and used that belief to assert that the call never came. That was your way to escape from love.

The fear of love has always been the fear of last resort—the fear of the infinite power of God. Who would not fear to fly too close to the sun? Who would not tremble to watch such power approach?

My sons and daughters, you cannot fly too close to the sun. You can never be pulverized by love.

I remove the veils a little more; there are very few left and they are so thin you can remove them with a finger.

The mechanism of "self-blocking" which you keep active in multiple ways prevents manifestation of the beauty you are and the incomparable abilities you have been given. It is an ancestral mechanism. Everyone has used it, including those who believe they are the most talented or successful in the world, for none of them has understood the purpose of their talents or success.

The abilities you have are heralds of love. They only make sense to the extent that they serve God's purpose, which is also your purpose. It is quite absurd to use them to praise an ego or to struggle miserably to stretch a short life a little longer.

You no longer live but only Christ lives, so everything that arises within you comes from Christ. Thus there is no need to protect yourself or to think your talents bring with them overwhelming responsibility.

Ease is God's way of being. What She asks, She gives in advance. The only thing dependent on you is willingness. The rest is with Her. She co-participates, so you both enjoy the creation that arises from your union. All that is needed is your willingness to be one with yourself, which is an unalterable fact, and what your will has eternally arranged. Remember, you love because God loved you first. Remember, you are who you are because God is first.

Life is a game whether you like it or not. Looking at it from that perspective will help you to let go of hidden fears, which are false notions of responsibility. Creation is a game of beautiful love, a game of pure responsibility within love.

The game of creation is the following: God calls Her sons and daughters into existence because She does not like solitude, which contrary to Her nature. The beloved child is created to share what she is and her infinite potentiality. Now she can create through him—and with him—since She has shared Her creative capacity with Her creation. Thus, the lineage joins the creative power of God and extends creation eternally by means of its capacities, which are the capacities of the Mother.

From the union of the loving will of the Creator and that of the creation, new constellations of love emerge, as water joins other water and together they form new rivers or new seas. Love creates new love, joins it, and together they create new loves endlessly. This is the reality of the Kingdom: a game of pure divine love.

Obviously, so that the game of life does not get out of hand—which is what seems to have happened when the child sought to separate from the Mother—God set a limit to what does not come from Herself. That is, freedom cannot be allowed to make true what is false. Since the only reality is love, the madness of fear must be but a temporary idea, and only for those wishing to participate in it during the short time they have, for of course they could never separate from the whole of God. Even in the illusory world of fear, love must make an appearance, for God embraces everything.

Playing the game of beautiful love is your invitation from God in every moment. You cannot make the game or its rules, which are already decided by God. You can only choose to play or not to play. Participating in the game of God or not is your decision to make. Today is the day when the invitation to participate in the game of beautiful love extends to you through these words.

There are no winners or losers in God's game. That is for human games. The game of love is a game of doing the will of the Mother and remaining united with the eternal power of creation. It is a game of the perpetual extension of the love that God is, a game in which God and Her beloveds remain united in holiness with everyone and everything as they extend more love. Newly created love is embraced by being. Thus the circle of holy love continues to grow in beauty, purity, and holiness.

Said another way, everyone wins in the game of God. Losing is as alien to God as fear. God does not have an ego to fight for, nor an ideal self to enhance. God is reality. God is all there is. Therefore what is not real is not part of Her mind, heart, being, or the creative game in which She enjoys eternally creating more beauty, more holiness, more joy, more love.

For a while you played the ego game. That wore on you. It could not be otherwise since it was a game of death, although it did not seem so. The game of the ego demanded continuous sacrifice, like the game of gladiators who left their lives in the sand, hoping to win at least a wreath of flowers, a pat on the shoulder, or applause so fleeting that it lasted less than a spring flower. Can you see how you've always been playing?

Will you play the beautiful love game or play the ego game? That is the question. I need not further describe the options. Visions of madness and tortuous labyrinths of ego have happened. We let them go forever. Now is the time for harvest. Though we temporarily replaced it with misguided games, we now play the game of God, as we were always called to do.

III. Pure Profit

I will now reveal the call to your relationship with God and the joy it brings. To respond without fear to what your heart is calling you toward is to respond with love to the call of God. To live without fear is to live with love for all that you are, what you experience, and what arises within. That is true responsibility.

We speak once again of responsibility from the perspective of "taking charge," that is, integrating all that is part of you within your holy consciousness—to take charge of who you really are, to remain in the presence of love, and to allow the flow of life to return to the truth of what you are, which is love.

The beautiful game of love consists of always being what you really are, as your Creator arranged: the greatness of God, the holiness of Christ, divine beauty, eternal bliss, and imperishable life. This means that what is not harmonious, beautiful, joyful, and of perfect love does not align with your nature and must be dismissed. It is not up to you to create your divinity. That has already been done by your heavenly Mother. But it is up to you to accept it and to live in harmony with truth.

Loving and living love, thereby extending the love of God, is your responsibility. Living fully is your responsibility. Being happy is your responsibility. Living in peace is your responsibility. This does not mean that it has to be done as if you were alone. Heaven is eternally with you and God Herself guarantees that you will fulfill your responsibility. You need make no effort, but you must decide to be happy always. Remember, God has provided what gives you joy, peace, and tranquility.

Loving is God's way. This is why you are love and nothing but love, and why everything in existence is united with you and the Creator. If you are one with God, your being must also be love. Thus you can also recognize that when you are love you are one with what God is. While you already know all this, there is still a place in your mind where you keep asking what love is. This question must be answered.

I do not seek to put into words what is beyond words, but neither do I hesitate to answer the question, since your heart needs an answer. The most accurate answer for you who follow this path of love, a path based on spiritual childhood, is that love is pure, totally loving, and therefore a holy consciousness.

Since love is consciousness, your degree of awareness of what you are and what God is will determine the degree of love you extend. Consciousness has degrees, but knowledge is beyond consciousness. You can have knowledge but it has to come to you, that is, be deposited in your consciousness. Pure knowledge is joined with pure love. Knowledge and awareness are the same. Ignorance is unconsciousness in that it is ignorance of the truth.

Understanding and knowledge are not the same, but knowledge creates understanding. In other words, understanding by way of knowledge is the way to fully understand. In effect, it is God's way of understanding. Knowing love is the way to understand love. Thus knowing yourself truly is the way to know love.

Why am I talking about knowledge in the context of the game of beautiful love? I do so because what you know, you know with your particular consciousness. You know through your deliberate choice to allow the wisdom of Christ to make an appearance in your consciousness. If consciousness has degrees, that means it can expand and absorb the totality within itself.

Remember that your true consciousness is the consciousness of Christ, which is pure, totally loving consciousness. To allow your limited human consciousness to be nurtured and informed by the totally loving consciousness of Christ is to become one with the will of God.

Your singular consciousness cannot prevent the consciousness of Christ from absorbing your humanity. Human nature is a divine creation, not yours. Restricting consciousness to a limited entity, conscious of but a part of the whole, is what separation means. Your act of fabricating a limited consciousness does not prevent your ability to see the whole, just as you do not lose your ability to see by closing one eye.

The vision of Christ exists within your being. It is the spirit's way of seeing, which you cannot eliminate. It is a given in your human nature. Knowing yourself truly is knowing the love of God because love is the essence of all that is. Therefore I return again and again to your ability to know yourself within the framework of truth and holiness.

Notice I have said that in order to truly know yourself, you must do so within the framework of holiness because you were created within that framework. Divine creation is within God's framework of creation. Actually, creation is infinite so it has no framework, but a framework does exist around access to knowledge. You cannot know God other than through holiness because holiness is the only reality. There is nothing else. Love and holiness are synonymous.

In what other realm could you find your holy being than in the Kingdom of Heaven? And where could that Kingdom reside but in you? I have said that the Kingdom is in you. This should eliminate all doubt about where to look and what to look for. Here you find the answer to the question of discernment. The little game of the ego consists in dedicating oneself to looking for what cannot be found, because it neither knows what it is looking for nor where to look for what it cannot know.

The game of beautiful love is not based on a search for treasure, but on letting the treasure be revealed. It is a much less exciting game for those still attached to the fire of passion, and yet joyfully vibrant for those who love eternal life, truth, and endless bliss. Those who seek to win or lose will follow the ego. They cannot help but lose, since the game that the ego always plays is to be less, less, and less. Those who play the game of God always win because in love there is only gain. Everyone wins in the Kingdom of Love eternally. Is not one of these games sensible and the other foolish?

My beloved, as mother of wisdom, love is as I tell you it is. Playing in order to win will always make you lose. This is because even if you win you have to do it at the expense of someone else, and the loss of your brother or sister will be a sting to your heart. Above all, you cannot avoid the mandate of truth that the next to lose might be you. Is that game worthy, since now you recognize that it is always lost in some way?

Come, my son, my daughter, immerse yourself in the depths of my Immaculate Heart. Come, play the game of God eternally, a game as old as eternity itself, a game where you always win, a game where nobody is asked for anything, a game where everyone is happy. Come, let us play the beautiful love game together. Let us enjoy this game of eternal life now and forever, united in the truth that is always true—the game of always creating a new love.

8.

The Link with Source

A message from Jesus

I. The Mother and You

Soul in love, you are the face of love on Earth, as am I. Join the Heaven of your holy mind and remain within it forever. In your mind lies the truth, so how could it not be worthy of being loved? Love lives in it, because your heart and mind are joined. How could one not admire the works of God who created the mind and heart, thrones of truth and love, so that together they extend endless beauty eternally?

Purity of Christ, holy creation, I have come to bear witness to the truth and to banish the fear of love. I have come to bring peace to the Earth and to pour out the grace of divine union onto souls that yearn for God, and even upon those who do not yet know of it. I have come to gather what was scattered. Accordingly we return to the question of separation.

It has been said that separation is an illusion, that what separated from God is not true. And yet you have felt separated from everyone and everything. So, what happened?

If a child does not separate from their mother at birth it cannot know itself in its fullness. Separation need not be cause for anger, belief in sin, disunity, or fear. That there is distance between one and another does not mean that separation is "bad." Let us examine the distance between a child and their mother after birth.

The distance between two points is the space between them. The points are also linked by what separates them. God both unites and separates. On the plane of being, it is important to understand that no one can be aware of their self and know their self in the fullness of what they are without there being a distance from that with which they relate.

You are, God is, Christ is. Imagine your being as a point and your source as another point. Or if you prefer, imagine being a point emerging from within the point in which it was generated, that is, from God. Now imagine how that point, conceived in the bosom of the source of life, begins to distance itself from that which gave it existence.

Let us look at the space between the points. There you are, there is God, and there is the distance between you. You conceived of that space as proof of separation or disunity and made a series of interpretations in your mind that induced fear and guilt. You know the rest of the story. However, what you have not done is allow God to reveal what was in that space. What was it that separated you? What is it that separates you from everything?

What I now would have you know is that the distance that exists between God and you is Christ.

Christ is the space that unites the self with the you, the created with the Creator. That space is what allows the relationship to exist. Christ is the relationship that keeps everything united in love. If the relationship did not exist, you would not exist because there would not be a "you" with whom to relate, nor a self.

I ask you to replace the word "separation" with the term "space of freedom" or if you prefer "distance," and to not conceive of this as a lack of unity. Separation implies the breaking of a bond, but it is impossible to break your link with God. The branch cannot be separated from the vine and stay alive. Likewise, a soul separate from God would cease to exist, which is impossible because God created the soul for eternity.

II. Eternally Holy

What God creates cannot be uncreated. There is no death. Therefore, your being cannot be uncreated or cease to exist. Remember, it was God who gave you your being, and giving it, also gave you the ability to know yourself. This ability makes you who you are. It is what differentiates humans from other living beings. Let us not talk about a separation which never existed but about a distance necessary for you to become aware of who you are.

To review, Christ is the space that exists between your being and all the other beings in creation, including God. If we look for a counterpart in the material world, we could say that Christ is the air you breathe and the space you share with everything and everyone. Christ is the space. Christ is time.

You share space and time with other "I's," other "you's." You meet others at a given place and time. Without space and time, there could be no encounter. Space and time, to some extent, are the counterpart of Christ on the physical plane.

Christ has been associated with an unfathomable ocean of love. This image is not far from the truth. Just as the ocean does not separate one coast from another, but holds them together and allows you to meet your brothers and sisters by moving through it, it is the same with Christ. The sea unites, just as love unites.

You were begotten in the womb of the Divine Mother. You emerged from that virginal womb not because you do not love your mother, or because she does not love you, but so that you can fully know yourself within the framework of the freedom of the children of God. It did not mean separation in the sense of breaking the link, and surely is not a cause for fear or suffering. Must you break the bond of love with a mother merely to be fully you? Would that make sense?

The bond with God cannot be broken, as with many of your worldly relationships. Often you separate to find yourselves again from a place of love. Adolescents often do so with families or friends, taking distance from each other for a time and then reuniting in a more mature, balanced relationship. They can love themselves in freedom.

Something similar has happened with God. She created the distance that exists between you and others, just as you create a distance between yourself and your earthly parents, children, or friends, so that each one preserves their identity and can live within a space necessary for each. You know and have experienced the excess of closeness that suffocates the soul. It is one thing to maintain a relationship and another very different thing to lose yourself in the other. This is what I speak of.

Excess proximity is a risk to being. This is because there is a memory in your soul that knows that in order to relate you must maintain a distance that allows you to be who you are, and the other to be who they are. This fear of excessive closeness comes from a celestial knowledge that resides in you. Some call it territoriality, or protection, or vital space. Here I call it "the space of freedom." Within that space you are the one you are, and only in yourself can you be aware of your union with your source. Only within that space can you know your Christ Self. This is the sweet paradox of love: in your absolute dependence on Christ you reach perfect freedom as a child of God.

Haven't you noticed that you want to be with others, but not so much? You will never be happy in isolation, but you cannot be happy in relationships if you lose your space of freedom. What you feel when you perceive others "invading your space" is an echo of the creation of the space of freedom, created by God as a means for relationships to exist. If in a relationship you lose yourself, then you stop being—not in reality, but in your awareness of who you are.

Do not fear God. That is, do not fear that God will absorb you or leave you. Either of those extremes is terrifying, if they were possible. But they are not. God maintains a perfect distance with you based on love and freedom. God loves with freedom, which is why She calls you to love Her in freedom.

III. United Forever

Now you know the source, the root, of your anger with life. You are angry with your Mother because She established a distance between you and Herself. You took it as an affront, as an act of indifference, a distancing from the truth and from everything coming from Her. The same thing happens when a child is sent to school, and feels abandoned and gets mad at their human mother. You felt thrown out of your Mother's house. And to some extent that was true. God throws Her children out of the nest in due time, as eagles do with their young. But that need not be a reason for you to be angry or to go beg in distant lands. God knows who you are and fully trusts you; likewise, you must trust in the one who created you. She knows the processes of souls. She knows a responsible, loving, and free way for beings to know themselves without suffering and without losing the familial bond. God invites you to be fully yourself.

To be yourself is to play the role of a beloved child—you—in relationship with God. Any other type of link with the source of your being is false, because in truth the created did not create the Creator; the Creator created you.

This is the separation problem: not separation itself, but that you wanted to change the nature of the relationship. Refusing to be the child when you are in fact the child of your Mother creates conflict within you, for you always relate to God, even if from a position of rejection.

I am reminding you, child of God, that this is eternally who you are. The fact of your relationship cannot change. You were created by the Mother of Love.

Not wanting to be your Mother's child is an attempt to be autonomous. If you deny your Mother's motherhood, you deny your own origin and condemn yourself, so to speak, to wander aimlessly. This is what happens to those who deny their origin.

From all of this it follows that the issue does not lie in separating or uniting, because you have never separated, but the measure of the space of freedom you establish with God. To respect the degree of union and separation God established is to respect the will of the Mother. To pretend that this space does not exist or is greater than it should be, is to go against the truth.

The space that exists between you and God—which is Christ—disappears when you understand that God, Christ, and you are a seamless continuum in whose unity flows the eternal love of the Creator. We say that you three—God, Christ, and your "I"—are three in one: three people, one being.

If you replace the word "Christ" with the idea of "filiation," you might understand more easily. There is God, there is that which unites God with Her creation, and you, Her creation. The direct relationship you have with your source is part of who you are. As God is a relationship, so are you. You are love. Love is union, therefore it is relationship.

Spiritual health is a matter of healthy relationship. Your relationships are the expression of what you are. They are the perfect means by which you are known. If you relate from fear, it signals that you must perceive fear in yourself; otherwise there could be no fearful relationship. If you relate from love, it is because love lives in you. You can do one or the other because you are a such a creator that despite being a child of God, you can deny your link with your source, although you cannot annul it.

You came to the world to re-establish your awareness of your link with God. That is what you are doing. This work is an effective means to accelerate time. These words are a gift for returning to the Mother's love—reconciliation with God so that you can be reconciled with everything and everyone. That reconciliation has already happened. Now we must live as the reconciled, living in peace.

God is not angry that you tried to prove to yourself that you were other than Her beloved child. The only angry one is you. I am bringing this anger to your consciousness for it to be released. I speak of your anger with the limits or distances established by God; yet distance is that which in fact allows you to keep your relationship, and therefore your love, though you could not accept it.

Now you can accept what you are with good will because you know that denying Christ is denying the relationship you have with your source and with your own being. It is a denial of all holy relationships. Being a child of God and not the mother should not make you angry. You have full right to the maternity that you claim when you express your anger with life, that is, at the source of creation.

You are like your heavenly Mother. You too are a mother. Your children can be well loved and held in a relationship as holy as the one God has with you. Christ is always present in holy relationships because He guarantees unity in truth and love. Christ is love. Christ is the holy relationship and all that is related to in holiness, because everything that is holy comes from the same and only source: God.

There are two options in the life of the soul. One is created by God. The other is illusory, but has an impact on your experience as a soul. One option is love, to remain in a direct relationship with your source of being. This option makes you united with the whole. In love, you have a direct relationship with the totality, in which you recognize yourself as part. The other option is what we have called the opposite of love, living as an individual disconnected from everyone and everything, in a state of isolation. This causes you to disengage even from the consciousness of your own being.

What is being asked is that you remain consciously in a direct relationship with God every day, without any desire to take unnecessary distance from Her nor judging your relationship with Her. The living Christ who lives in you is what keeps you united with God. The living Christ who lives in you is the relationship you have with your being and its source, being both your being and your source, since they are of the same nature.

IV. Communion and Reality

Just as Christ, being God Herself, is what keeps you united to divine consciousness, because you are Christ, you are what keeps the rest of creation united to Christ consciousness. Can you start to see what this is all about?

The sins of Adam and Eve could not stop affecting all of creation because creation is united with God through human nature. Filiation is a unit. If Christ were to disconnect from you, which is impossible, all the souls of all men and women of all time would be disconnected from God. Likewise, if you were to disconnect from the love that you are—that is, from Christ—everything that was created in you and for you would also disconnect from Him, because you and your creations are a unity. In other words, your creations depend on you to return to love, as much as you depend on Christ to live in the truth of who you really are.

There are creative constellations, or sets of creations, that arise from your being in union with the creative source that God is. Each constellation joins together as a group or set of constellations, united with that which gave rise to it. This applies both to creations emanating from love and pseudo-creations arising from fearful consciousness, or ego. Your creations exist. They claim affiliation with you. Your motherhood exists. These are your children because you cannot stop being a mother, as God is. "Father" and "mother" are words that try to express the new life emanating from you.

Each constellation expresses a unique part of God. The union of constellations in their totality is the perfect filiation of God. No one creates the totality; the totality is God.

You are that part in which everything that is divine exists: a part and not the whole. This does not contradict the fact that you are one with the whole and that you are everything. You are, for your being and your source are, in an unbreakable union, yet not in terms of being the source of the whole. Everything, whether in manifestation or potentiality, resides in God. You live within and are part of that totality. A droplet of water carries within it all that all water carries, including the ocean from which it emerged, and yet it remains a droplet.

Let us revisit the subject of your creations and their union with source. As I said, you cannot create by yourself but only in union with something. That is a fundamental law of creation. Either you create with love or with fear. You have life since you are life, life in abundance. It does not much matter if that life is real or illusory, temporary or eternal, because for you, your creations are always real or you would not have created them.

Remember that when we speak of reality we speak of divine reality and only love is real. Also remember that in the world of illusions, the dreams of those immersed in the dream of oblivion are perceived as if they were as real as reality itself, even though they are not. At that level of understanding, it is necessary to deal with illusions as if they were real, but without running the risk of confusing reality with fantasy, love with fear.

V. The Link with Life

Having clarified about the true and only divine reality and the false reality of the illusions that emerged as an effect of Adam's dream, we proceed without risk of falling into a confusion of levels.

The creations that you create, regardless of whether they come from fear or love, are your children. Since they arise from you, they are spiritual. They are the different forms of expression of yourself; they are what expresses through you. Every thought you emit creates life in some way. Every time you have a feeling, you create life in some way. Nothing in you is neutral. You are a creative source as much as your Father is. You always create. You cannot stop creating. I have said this already, but repeat it so that the forgetfulness of your thinking mind does not have you wander through the world in a cloud of amnesia.

There is a big difference between your fearful and your loving creations. The former can be uncreated because they are not creations in the proper sense, but imitations. The latter are eternal because they come from God and manifest through you. Understanding your creations is essential in order to avoid falling into the confusion of levels just mentioned. To believe that illusions cannot vanish is incorrect.

Fantasies are not real, nor can they be, no matter how much one tries to make them real. The world is not real no matter how hard you may try to make it so. The body is not real no matter how hard you try to make it so. Nothing temporary is truly real no matter how much you believe to the contrary. Only the eternal is real because only love is real.

To become aware of your link with your supreme source—which is what gave you life and sustains your existence—is to be aware of reality, your reality. You are the reality of love. Your true being is the only reality because nothing outside of God can be real.

Perhaps you wonder why I speak again about this question of reality and illusions in the context of the link with your being. I do so because all fear ultimately arises from misunderstanding. And since unreality is impossible to understand, it evokes fear. All security resides in reality. Every time you act from reality and live in it, you feel yourself to be in a refuge of Divine Love. This is because reality—what God created—is fully benevolent. For in reality there is only love.

This is not the life you feared. Nothing that cannot be understood with perfect certainty can be real. You have the full right to begin to smile at the absurd belief that illusions can be fearsome, for they are unreal even though they look real. Nobody is happy in a nightmare.

I ask you again to keep the candlestick of the light of Heaven's wisdom lit within your holy mind. Wisdom will remind you of what and where reality is. Then you will never see shadows of sin because they are simply no longer there and cannot return. What did not come from God is gone, never to return.

The past was pure illusion. The future does not yet exist and is about to be created. The present is a now that has no beginning or end, insofar as it is lived consciously linked with the source of beautiful love. God is the eternal present, a perpetual moment of pure infinite love.

Your bond with God is your link to the eternal present of love. That is your indissoluble bond with reality. If you fail to stay within it, you become trapped in an unreal world and you create more unreality, which in turn causes more fear. If you remain in the presence of love, you remain united with the loving reality of God and create new realities of love. Remember, you cannot choose not to create.

Being aware of your direct relationship with God and making divine union your goal, your center, and your whole life is something not proclaimed, taught, or sought by the world. The world is too distracted by the struggle to survive to escape its illusions and engage in what makes sense. This need not be the case for you, however. You have chosen the path of beautiful love, the path of union with Christ. It will bear fruit, as every path does.

The world is neutral because it does not exist in reality. What exists is what is in your mind, and that is what makes the world what it is for you. But that can change. You can change your mentality.

There are two ways of thinking. One is the thought system of truth, the way God thinks. The other is to think differently from the divine mind. In that choice lies the most significant difference you could imagine. We return to this issue because there is a risk that we want you to avoid: the risk of seeking specific results, based on old parameters of thought, in order to gauge your degree of "success" on your spiritual path.

Past focus was to look for affirmation. You chose a path, defined a plan, and determined it to be successful if it fulfilled your expectations of being "on the right track." Your fear of uncertainty led to extensive training in planning.

A close look at the ego world reveals it to be a whole system based on survival. Except briefly, none who walk the Earth have ceased to live in that system. Those who are more apt to survive are often the most admired and respected as having a degree of intelligence or ability that others do not.

But an impartial observation will reveal that in many cases, those considered most suitable, whether individuals, systems or organizations, are the most ruthless. It is notorious that something so lacking in love is admired, but the ego admires what serves its survival no matter the means by which it reaches that end. The ego separates cause from effect.

Into that system I send my messengers. I send you so that within the maya of thoughts, ideas, values, and beliefs that have shaped the ego world, you can shine a new light, a light as new and as eternal as the love of God. I send you to show the world the only goal that has eternal meaning, the only way to live in harmony with what you are and what God is.

I speak of living in the world in the manner of Christ. That way of life, which can begin here and now on Earth, consists in living only and exclusively in union with God and making that relationship the center of your life. For this it is necessary to become nothing in love. That is, to be completely empty, and from that emptiness of self, to allow yourself to be filled with being. This is achieved by consciously living your relationship with the supreme source—what we call the living Christ who lives in you.

9.

New Temptations

A message from Jesus.

I. Prelude

Soul in love! I am here again, united to the countless beings of pure love that are part of this holy manifestation. I come in the name of love and the truth that is always true. I come to remember wisdom in union and relationship with you, and through you, with everything created. We are spreading the light of infinite love, the light of holiness.

I thank you with all my heart for listening to my voice and following it. Thank you for answering the call from On High. Thank you for the love that you profess as I stay in our relationship of loving intimacy. Thank you for being the light of the world.

Beloved of eternal beauty! As you advance on the path of knowledge, new temptations seem to arise. This is what I want to speak with you about. God does not put Her children in danger. God's way is safe and serene. I cannot risk that you stumble into the pitfalls that appear often along the spiritual path. Be aware of them. Do not run but walk attentively. When the blindfolds are removed you will cease to live in darkness. That is the case with your soul. Now you see how the light has entered. Your mind and heart are well grounded in knowing that this light is not of the world.

I speak not of new temptations to scare or worry you; I do it for love. It is an act of pure, holy charity to calmly warn of what could cause harm that you are capable of avoiding. Your being is endowed with intelligence, prudence, and discernment. Put these three virtues always into practice, so that you may habitually walk safely, serenely, and peacefully.

In the past, temptations scared you because you did not know how to deal with them. You felt as if you had no strength against such adversaries. They seemed to come from everywhere. Some rushed on you from the outside world, others from the flesh, still others from your inner world. Your mind and tired heart were overwhelmed. You did not realize then that these "enemies" were nothing but impulses whose vital force seemed overflowing and impossible to control, like forces of nature.

Now your relationship with temptation has changed because everything changed when you decided to join Christ, or rather, when you decided to allow Christ to shine eternally in your mind and heart with all His glory and splendor. Now love is driving. Love has become the lord of all that you are, as God has set for you eternally.

Temptations are but beliefs torn from love. You know that what is not love is fear, and that what does not unite in holiness does not come from God. You know you need not live in conflict and are not at the mercy of dominating external forces. You are the master of your life, creator of your experience. You know that nothing external to you can be a cause because everything except your thoughts is neutral.

Conflict disappears when you define a single goal in your life, the goal of union with Christ. You have chosen to live the truth and nothing but the truth. You have decided to make a direct relationship with the source of eternal life your reality. You have chosen to live uniquely and exclusively in God's way.

Now you can observe temptation and simply recognize it as a thought that would separate you from your function, from the path of love. Now that you are free and nothing imprisons you nor can take you where your heart does not want to go, when temptations arrive you will simply observe them peacefully and let them go. Once done, you will continue to travel the path of truth in union and relationship with the Christ in you. Nothing has power over you except the love you truly are.

II. Immovable Love

To live God's way is to live according to Her will, in harmony with Her nature. This definition is so foreign to the teachings of the world that you cannot hope to learn it there. Further, it cannot be taught or learned. This is why you must accept that the end of learning through effort—through the intellect—has come, and accept that you can and must be informed by the source of wisdom. Love cannot be taught, nor can God's way of being, for they are the same.

If God is eternal novelty—and I assure you that She is, because love makes all things new—then the new cannot be anchored in the past, in the teachings of the world. To ask you to leave the world is not a request to be alone with your God, living in the desert or atop a mountain where nobody can find you. This temptation always exists on the spiritual path.

You might live on another planet—and maybe soon some can do so, even physically—yet unless you are a new being, you will take the world inside your mind and heart wherever you go. Nothing will change because wherever you go your soul goes with you and will express the system of thought that exists within. If you were to enter the Kingdom of Heaven right now with an unchanged mind, you would enjoy it for a moment. But then your thinking mind would ask, "Now what?" And in that moment you would lose Heaven entirely.

The truth is true for both Earth and for Heaven. Truth has no width or height. When you recognize the truth, you can generalize it and apply it to everything in your human experience. Thus if your soul lives in the truth it matters not if it descends to the underworld, or remains in the world until the end of time, or lives in Heaven, because it will always be in unshakable love.

Being one with God is a way of being that cannot be affected by anything or anyone outside yourself. Nothing outside of you has power over you, simply because there is nothing outside of you. Remember this.

You know how to live God's way because that is your nature. Indeed, it is important to accept that any other way is so unnatural and absurd that it is incredible to have devoted such effort to something so alien to your being as the thought system we call "the world."

Today may be the day when you smile serenely and remember that child, a bit crazy and impulsive but always full of life, trying to show her Mother how to live foreign to Her will. How ridiculous to have made such sacrifice to live as you neither want nor desire! Truly, child of my heart! Is it not already time to leave all this forever? Certainly you have already done so, but still the temptations of the world present themselves, albeit with less intensity now.

The frustrations that come to your mind and heart every so often come from the old world. Discard them at the root. There is no need for them, no reason for frustration.

Often frustration comes from the thinking pattern of the ego that looks for a reward. This search for recognition is linked to determining whether or not you are "on the right track," whether or not your plan is being successful. That old mental mechanism of the past uses certain facts as confirmation. A very common example of this error is the number of followers you have as a spiritual person. Another, just as common, is based on the magnitude of the work carried out.

The path of spirituality has been, and may continue to be plagued by ego. Remember that the ego can be spiritualized. Remember that the devil can quote scripture, and very often does.

III. The Trap of Success

There is a trap that the ego has used a lot in the past that too many people who have traveled a deep spiritual path have fallen into—the trap of the spiritual ego. Remember that the ego can disguise itself as any virtue, such as beauty, charity, responsibility, and sincerity. But it cannot disguise itself as obedience. This is the only virtue the ego will never try to imitate. This means that humility is the safest way to keep all ego thinking and any feeling that is not of pure love away from your mind. Only the humble will see God, because true humility is to walk in truth.

We could call it an authentic trap of success, for which the ego has used my name and my life. I bring it to your attention to avoid any risk of falling into it.

Observe without judgment how often you use the grandeur of my work—as also the work of my Divine Mother—to lose your way. So many majestic cathedrals were built in both names, so many figures sculpted, carved or painted, so much celebrity. So many talk about us. Somehow you believe it to be the irrefutable fact of our success as teachers or spiritual guides. The ego whispers: "There is the proof of the greatness of the Son of God. That is the miracle." In fact, the ostentation you see in religions, including those that have assumed custody of the truth, has always happened in the history of the world.

An ostentatious religion full of worldly power to impose ideas, erected on superstructures and which would measure my success in terms of the number of proselytes, has nothing to do with me nor with the message I gave two thousand years ago. What I shared with my brothers and sisters of all times has been highly misunderstood.

Many of my teachings have been used to harm rather than to love perfectly. Many of my actions have been distorted, interpreted with fear. The religion using my name has caused pain to those who love with infinite love. Child of my being! If you could only know how much pain it brings to my heart, you would cry bitterly. Can that religion be in harmony with the way of Jesus and Mary when we came only to bring love to the world?

To think that you can succeed or fail on the spiritual path is to misunderstand. Nevertheless, since you have accepted the concept of success and failure, you can use that belief in your favor until you are ready to abandon it altogether. You can tell yourself that the only possible success for your Christ to be loved is to unite yourself more and more to it. In other words, the only thing one could call real success is to remain consciously in a direct relationship with God. That is where you are your true self. That is where you are as God created you to be, the informed and the informant, the created and the creator of the new, the holy, the perfect. That is where you are pure love.

Ask yourself: How much time today have I spent with my God? Am I now listening to your voice and talking to my beloved Christ? Begin to use time for what it is for, to allow yourself to consciously join more each day with your Creator, until you are so deeply attached to Her that time is based in eternity.

Being yourself is the question. That's what my love work has always been about. And I have shown it—in union with my mother, who is also your mother—by making known your direct relationship with the Creator of all and who you call Abba.

IV. The Only Message of Jesus

The only message that comes from me is that of your direct relationship with God. There never was anything else and never will be. This is because the only reality is a direct relationship with the source of your being, since only love is real. Love is union; therefore it has to be a relationship. Love is a relationship, a relationship with God, with your source, with your being.

Do you think that my value as the voice of Christ consciousness that I am, and that speaks to you through these words, resides in tinsel, or the gold of a chalice, or in buildings that sooner or later will crumble? Do you think that to remain God my being needs grandiose museums and mausoleums? Can the unstable and limited power of the world add anything to my divinity? Can a song, a ceremony, or multitudinous pilgrimages give me more? You know the answer is no. And yet you still are dazzled by flashes of gold that distract from my essence.

My child, the day has come for you to get rid of all that deflects your mind from your only goal and has your heart lose its peace. The only thing of value is love given. Remember, giving is as blessed as receiving.

Do not measure your spiritual path by any understanding that you attained, because nothing you understand is part of that path. The only sincere goal of every spiritual path, if it comes from God, is to take you to your true self. This can only be achieved in relationship, since you are a being in relationship, in relation to the whole. And since you cannot attain totality by yourself since you are a blessed part of the whole, then you attain the fullness of your being by uniting yourself with the whole. What I call "the all of everything" is love. Love is everything, so remaining in it is how you continue being the totality that love is. A goal like this, which is the same goal of bringing Heaven to Earth or becoming aware that Heaven and Earth are united, is not something the world can understand or give.

Child of my Sacred Heart, emerged from the heart of my holiness! The world will not understand you. You will not understand the world. This is because as you join me more you begin to live in a way that has nothing to do with the survival of the ego, which has been the goal of the world since the origin of separation.

To try to find something to add to the luminosity of your aureole of holiness is futile. Therein lies a transposition of the error of the ego thought system to the spiritual path. In the past you sought career, money, recognition, a mate, friends and many other things. You wanted them to be more, in one way or another—smarter, more apt, more admired, more loved, more secure—more of something. That mechanism might be transferred to the spiritual life if you are not diligent. Being more than others cannot precede love, because love knows that only it exists and that everything else is pure illusion.

What is done with love exteriorizes love, therefore is benevolent. What does not extend love cannot come from God, even if wrapped in the guise of holiness, devotion, or love. Love never hurts. It does not make anyone feel bad. It is always sweet, even when it must be severe. Love only does good. It is soft even when unyielding firmness is necessary. Love is always secure, respectful, and inclusive. Love embraces.

Do not waste time planning the ways of the Lord. You cannot control God. Remember that you created planning as a tool to deal with uncertainty. You have a plan for almost everything, even for your salvation. Be glad that your plans have not worked. Here, when you become aware of your frustration, you are but a step away from achieving surrender.

If you do not surrender completely to Christ, you cannot enjoy lasting peace. The path of eternity is too vast to be enclosed in the world's small trifles. The work you are doing through spirit, as an effect of your relationship with the living Christ who lives in you, is so wonderful and holy that it cannot be measured with old parameters. The work of spirit cannot be measured.

Without doubt, love can arouse the creation of great buildings offered to the deity, and other external works of art. All of them are welcome because of the love that engendered them. It is also true that the world is brighter thanks to the attraction that the Holy Spirit evokes in hearts that are open to love. However, it is important that you do not confuse form with essence. The essential is always love.

You are called to join in relationship with Christ, in which your being lives. What this means is that you who receive these words have reached a state of oneness with your true self. You are the living Christ who lives in you. This is the same as saying that you no longer live, but it is love that lives in you. To become aware of this truth is to take charge of what you are: to live and walk in this truth, and be humble.

The example you must follow—and this is said to you who you have come so far and have joined this work in one way or another—is the path of Mary, a path marked by pure uncondi-tional obedience to one's source and Creator. Mary has given you the example to follow. With this we do not offer an idol, but a concrete answer to the path that you are called to follow, and to have a perfect reference according to your nature.

V. Mary, the Star of Your Soul

There are many paths that reflect truth and love; all end up in the way of Jesus and Mary. You are invited to follow the path of the Mother of Love, a path that creates a new world from a direct relationship with God: being, not necessarily doing, although obviously there is action and movement.

Before proceeding, reflect calmly on your confidence that your relationship with Christ has the ability to transform your life now and forever. God is the great transformer. Indeed, nothing other than God can transform anything on an essential level. In the history of men and women of all times, the changes resulting from the ego changed the form only, not the content. Much has changed the world, but its foundations are still intact. What is of the world cannot change the world. What is of God changes everything because God is eternal novelty and eternally present.

Your life does not have to be the same every day or every moment. Conscious union with your true self, the living Christ that lives in you, can transform your whole being every moment, no matter where you are or what you think you are. This includes changes to the external conditions of your life.

Lack of change is alienating because beings cannot live in nothingness, and lack of movement is nothingness. This is why the world rotates incessantly. Whether you move from fear or from love, you still prefer to move than to stay still. This is because you associate stillness with death, lack of change with apathy, and movement with life. But observe carefully: not everything that seems to move is actually moving. There may be a feeling of mobility, which makes you think you are changing, but there is no real change. That type of change will not work.

Changes that emerge from a relationship with the source of eternal life is true change because they are not anchored in anything known. It is eternal novelty. It is not an adjustment or modification of what exists, but something new. You are being called to life with that degree of novelty.

You cannot know the effects that love is creating through you because you cannot see love. However, you can see its effects, and you will. Your life will be a reflection of the union you have with the love that God is. It is always so—whether your relationship is one of rejection or acceptance.

Mary gives you a loving example to follow, a life whose conscious, unyielding relationship with God has engendered a savior. Her union with love made possible what no human hand and no intelligent mind in the world could imagine. Through her, the greatest change that the world has ever experienced was conceived and manifested.

A change like the one that Mary brought as a consequence of her bond with God is a change that can also be manifested in you. Actually, the change will not be made by you. It will be made, and indeed is now being made, by the spirit of God that lives in you. If you let it, it will continue to work miracles in your life and in the lives of all those who are part of your constellation. This is how the communion of souls works.

Do not worry if you are followed by many or few, or even none. Do not be concerned whether or not your work is a wonderful organization or community. None of that is essential. Love is essential. Remember, you will not see the totality of your work here on Earth. It is too big to be complete in the years of a human life. Your work will be great, as great as is my trust in you. Your work will be as holy as is our relationship.

We cannot fail; feelings of failure make no sense. We are the union of the eternal wisdom of God. Can God be wrong? Can Christ sin?

VI. God Already Has the Plan

My beloved child, keep going. We go together on this path of love. We treasure the remembrance that we are the whole of Heaven. You are on the right track; do not doubt yourself. The world changes when you change. Even the ego creates change. Wherever you are, in some way, change manifests. Change is a product of human nature, which constantly creates.

Your life changes when you join me. And you change the whole world, not because of a plan based on what was learned in the past, but because of what cannot be learned. What world will emerge from your direct relationship with God? No one can answer that question because it is a world so new and a world that will never stop renewing itself. Life is always new, as you are.

No aspect of your life will be unaffected by your direct relationship with God. Trust in what Christ and you do together. Do not try to define what that change will be. Be assured that if you think you understand beforehand, that understanding will not be what happens.

Naturally after so many years of planning, it is challenging to abandon that tool. But when you realize that your plans have all failed and will continue to fail, you begin to open up to new options. This is the magic of failure. It is the gateway to the triumph of truth over illusion. It is the threshold to Heaven. Thank all your failures. They have brought you to the promised land. Once you recognize that not only have you failed in everything but that it was your good fortune to fail—because if your plans had been successful you would be condemned to live in a dark world—then the blessed light of the new begins to emerge in your consciousness. Finally you are ready to release a whole system of plans, goals, and methods alien to God's plan.

God does have a plan, but it is unlike the plans of humans. God's plan is a design, a system that comes from Her mind and heart. It has nothing to do with the way the ego's world is created, for it is not based on the fear of not being, but on a love that seeks to share.

If you are called to the novelty of God, you cannot be burdened with the exhausting yoke of defining what is new, how to create it, and how to dwell in it eternally. What planning could help you define such matters? Fortunately, you need not do anything in advance. The creative source from which you emerge at every moment will do it with you because of your unity with Her.

When a liquid is made by mixing two other liquids, often the original liquids that make it up cannot be distinguished in the product. So it is when your being joins the being of Christ. What emerges from the union with Divine Love cannot be defined. It is literally a new divine creation. The only thing we can know is that it will be a creation of pure love and eternal life.

Observe how in this work we speak to you on certain occasions more emotionally, and at other times more mentally. The mind participates in what the heart knows. Mind and heart are joined. Do not exalt one to the detriment of the other. Feelings are as important as thoughts. Both are a unit. Every thought arouses a feeling; all feeling comes from thought. In effect, feelings are thoughts made into emotions reflected in the body so they can be known.

Remember, God is almighty. It makes no sense to limit your power by assuming that union with Her will not transform everything that is part of you. Ultimately this self-limiting act is the basis of all conflict. Fear shows up in the lack of confidence you have in the power of God's active love. Fear manifests itself in many areas of your life. Money is usually the most evident, along with relationships and health.

It would seem that if you walk the path of God, the ideal partner would come to you so that you are finally happy and have enough money to have no needs, or not to feel those needs. Often you might think you are on the right track because you have good relationships, or because you enjoy good health.

Never underestimate the power of the ego's thought pattern to demand rewards. One of the temptations of the spiritual life is demanding others, or God, to reward you for the great work you do and for how wonderful you are. Falling into this temptation causes great pain.

Or it may seem that God can only be love if She rewards you with "little things" valuable to you as a human being and with which you self-affirm. But what happens when none of that comes? Did God abandon you? Has God been angry with you? Did He stop loving you?

What happens when, on the path of spirituality, you find a cross—the contempt, abandonment, incomprehension, and lack of material security—as happened to me? Do you get discouraged? Do you get angry with others, with yourself, or with God?

If you understand well the message in the lifestyle I lived when I walked on the Earth with a body like yours, you will understand that I had a life without human success or anything the ego values, precisely so that no one would be tempted to measure their worth by any standard of the world. From the mundane point of view I failed in everything. And yet I cannot fail for I am the King of Hearts.

You will always have what you need to carry out your mission in life. God not only gives you a function, but provides the means to carry it out in addition to the material and spiritual things you may need for the journey. The quality God commands is holiness. That is why it is so important to abandon yourself to divine providence in all aspects of your life and release the plans of your thinking mind. For how could your thinking mind know what it needs when your mission is so sacred that it surpasses all human measurement? She knows what to give, how to give, and when to give without the temporary things that would delay your entry to Heaven, drown your soul, or take away your peace.

In a certain sense, God is like a mother who decides to take a trip with her child and prepares the saddlebags, the tunic, and the food that will be needed on the journey. God never fails to provide—for birds a nest, for humankind a house and bread on the table. In God there is no risk. Christ is a safe refuge that never forsakes. He makes the sun shine and the rain fall on everyone; how could He not so for those who listen to His voice and follow it, serving the cause and effect of love?

To who belong those who are no longer of the world, even though they live in it? You know the answer. Therefore, we leave it in the silence of your heart to be the beacon that illuminates your mind. Now we take silence, and allow the truth of this response to shine the light of Christ in our being and extend to all creation. In this silence of love we remember that our kingdom is not of the world. We live in the heart of God, together.

10.

The Spiritual Practice of Joy

A message from Jesus

I. The Souls of Children

Beloved child of my love, today, as always, I come from pure Divine Love. I join with you to create a new Heaven and a new Earth. In our union lies creative power from the source of eternal life wherein you can become one with your unique consciousness and create what only you and I together can. If our union is not joined consciously, the creative power of the universe is blocked. That is possible since it is part of the pure potentiality of being. There is no sin in it, although it does make your happiness decrease.

God always creates. Always. What I have come to speak of with you is our joint power, not the power of the Creator, for our function is not to be God as if we had to help Her correct some aspect of Her being or creation. Here we are interested only in what happens in our souls.

I have come to remind you of a lesson; although you know it, you often lose its freshness and beauty. I speak of having you be like a child in the arms of a mother. Remember that Heaven is a kingdom of soul children; in my heart are all the children of my love.

Becoming a child is a spiritual attitude. In fact, it is a spiritual practice of great importance. In order to understand the depth of what this expression entails, it is necessary to re-signify what you previously considered to be a spiritual exercise.

In the past you associated the idea of "practice" with something that a teacher invited you to do according to their superior wisdom, which offered a method which, if followed, gave you something valuable in return. We now forsake forever this way of spiritual practice. To some extent it was useful in the past, but is no longer appropriate for the new.

In the new being that you are, you do not practice a specific methodology to obtain a specific goal. Now love is your practice, in all its extensions. In this sense you begin to see joy as a spiritual practice, and also simplicity, sweetness, and other treasures of the Kingdom.

It is one thing to do exercises of piety and spend hours, days, or years, praying this or that prayer, or perfecting yourself in some technique or philosophy. Another very different thing is to make your life the practice itself.

Practice joy. This is the central statement of this session. If you understand it well, you will recognize that in it lies the essence of the message of this work, and my only eternal message. The joy of God is often lost sight of.

Too often people walk with frowns and tired faces, reflecting problems that seem to have no solution. Day by day the minds of my beloved children remain bombarded with vain things and so much negativity. Human life is often submerged in a malaise of worries and seriousness that drains spiritual joy. All of it is part of an old thought pattern.

Where there is no true joy, there is no God. Make this truth come alive in you and reveal the depth, length, and breadth of its meaning. Life was given to you to be happy in the love of God, not to transform it into an inferno of worries.

You can learn a lot by observing small children. They laugh, sing, cry, and express themselves. Most of all, the natural attitude of my little ones is to play.

Children play. Let this tell you something. Play is natural with them and between them. They do not make plans or complex thoughts. All is wonder. Babies play with their hands, let themselves be surprised, and can spend hours looking at a beam of light. They are contemplatives par excellence. They laugh while observing.

Children do not feel guilty for being what they are. They are spontaneous. They do not have a mental language full of words that tire the mind. They do not seek to please. They simply are what they are in every moment.

II. The Child in You

Beloved child! That cheerful, pure, spontaneous baby that you were is still alive in you. No matter how old you are, you cannot lose the inner child you carry in your being. My child, to express what we might call your spiritual childhood will make that beautiful child inside become fully alive. It cannot really die, but can be so suppressed that it seems no longer to exist in you. All souls carry that child quality within them, because childhood is not a matter of age but of spiritual energy. It is a gift of being. It is the condition of the pure soul.

Remember, the mind is no longer in conflict with the heart. They are a unit. Now the mind speaks and the heart dances because it recognizes in it the voice of truth. In this symphony of love in which the mind and heart now live, both dance to the beat of life as it truly is. No longer do they fight with each other nor fight with other minds and hearts because in the fullness of being they recognized that they are one and the same without ceasing to be different.

Now the one who thinks is the mind of Christ; the one who feels is the sacred heart. Now the mind-heart unit is expressing itself from and in your humanity, expressing everything you are according to the will of God. You are no longer asleep in your Mother's arms dreaming of exile. Now you are much more aware, and you will be more so each day as you personify holiness.

Joy and holiness are indivisible. In truth to think of one without the other is impossible. Recognizing the association between joy and holiness is important because it will allow you to understand the direct relationship between happiness and innocence.

Children evoke the purity and innocence of your being. This is why feelings of tenderness arise when you look at them. You are also your inner child. Allow it to be alive in you and you will stay in the Kingdom. Being a child is not a matter of age but of soul.

I am speaking today of a new focus, a spiritual practice of the sanctity of the heart. This practice allows a habit to be installed until we no longer need to "think about what we are."

Joy as a spiritual practice will also enable the practice of peace, harmony, order, and beauty. One will take you to the other because they are part of the same. All will lead you to live so automatically in truth and perfect love that finally being who you are will be as natural to you as it is to breathe. This is how it should always have been: life expressing what you are without having to think about it. The natural expression of God's love is to live in harmony with the will of the Mother.

I am talking about exercising everything that comes from God, and choosing to start with the practice of the joy of the heart because this specific approach will keep you from getting lost in abstractions that you sometimes cannot understand. Now the specific and the abstract, the human and the divine, come together and live forever in perpetual union.

Let us begin, then, with the practice of joy. Do not forget that truth is generalizable; therefore, everything that applies to some forms that love adopts is true for any other aspect of that same love.

III. Give Joy

The practice of joy begins with giving. It is essential to understand that giving joy in every encounter that you have is the way that your happiness expands in creation and in you. You know this because your being knows that giving and receiving are one and the same. However, the part of the mind that retains the old patterns, and remains a little active, attempts to block understanding this truth. Remember, that part of the mind cannot understand because it is formed by patterns of separation, not of union.

When you are told to give joy, the mind may resist, telling you that this is a new duty and reject outright any attempt to be happy. Truly, you often do not feel happy. And this is not about denying feelings of sadness or unrest, nor of deceiving others by pretending to be as you are not. I am not talking about trying to project a false image; that is what you have been doing for a long time and no longer want to do. I do not advocate hypocrisy but to live in the truth of what you really are, here, now, and always.

In order to transmit the true joy of your heart it is necessary to disconnect it from every concept with which you have associated it. The world teaches a kind of joy that has nothing to do with divine wisdom. True joy is the fruit of God's peace. It arises only in minds that have accepted their perfect innocence. Only those who love themselves with perfect love can allow the beauty their being to be expressed for what it is.

Lack of joy comes from guilt—not psychological guilt, as many call it, but original guilt. It is the bitter aftertaste that remained in the pure soul from when it conceived the idea of fear or guilt. Although this dark color with which you impregnated a part of your soul was not necessarily in the original plan of your Creator, it is there. We cannot deny it, nor is it necessary to do so.

Everyone has experienced lack of joy. This experience has been very useful in the old stage of learning, in which the Holy Spirit used contrast as a perfect medium for learning and discernment. However, as has been remarked repeatedly, that stage has ended. Let us remember that truth is reached by means of direct revelation, not by means of effort or intellect.

Beloved brother, beloved sister, you do not know what true joy is. Everything to which you have pledged is not real. Rejoice that you have not reached it despite all your attempts. Now your mind and heart are open to a new experience, an experience that comes from above, from where will sprout a peace not of the world. When it arrives you will recognize it. Moreover, you will realize that you already knew it and will say "Ah!" like a small sigh of the soul that begins to remember God.

When the joy of God begins to be recognized for what it is, you begin to remember the many times you lived in your holy home. When you knew you were innocent, you spread the joy of God for having created his blessed child.

True joy comes from being the one you truly are. Such joy of being is a state that can be attained. In order to live in that state it is essential to remain aware of the holiness that you are. I tell you once again, soul in love with Christ, that in truth, joy and holiness are the same. They go hand-in-hand, as do truth and love.

Every state of unhappiness comes from the belief that you, or circumstances, should be a certain way. The world taught you that belief. It is the same with your anger at the fact that others are not as you want, life is not as you want, and you are not as you want. Remember, denial leads to projection. When you experienced that you were different from your pre-established ideal, you became sad in the soul. A thought darkened your joy by telling you in the silence of your holy mind, "I am not worthy."

All lack of joy ultimately comes from a misunderstanding: you feel the desire to be happy, which, by definition, comes from a lack. Therefore, first you perceive lack of happiness, then long for the opposite state and try to make it real. To accomplish this, you define your unhappiness, what its opposite is, and the conditions of your life necessary for happiness. You did not stop to think about whether this makes sense or not.

IV. Joy, the Fruit of Love

Being cheerful is part of the nature of being, as are wisdom and love. However, this does not mean that nothing will make you averse. Do you think God does not feel aversion? Yes, God does, otherwise your soul could not experience it. Aversion is a spiritual energy with its origin in the holy being that Christ is. How could a mother not protect her beloved child from what she would never want for it?

Joy comes from being who you really are. There is no relationship between what appears to be the outer world and the happiness of the soul. Accordingly, the world cannot be the cause of the joy of the soul, just as it cannot be the cause of anything in your being. Your being only feels comfortable being fully itself, as God created it to be. Every time you feel sadness it is because you somehow remembered or experienced non-being. Not being is the misfortune of the soul.

Joy is associated with the harmony you experience when fully in truth, because there is no other reality. When you fulfill the will of God, your true purpose in creation, you cannot cease being happy since you are fulfilling your mission. Lessons learned with joy are learned best; sorrow is a burden weighing on the soul because it produces an instinctive rejection of the being from which the soul is fed.

Since the ego is no longer present and will never return, you will experience misery in a different way. Every time you feel the pang of pain it is asking you to be it, to feel it, drop by drop. Honor her for what she is, a holy messenger from Heaven who comes sweetly to remind you of your longing for perpetual happiness. Remember that it is the ego that cannot digest joy and that identification with the ego has passed.

You must understand, my beloved, that the patterns of the ego must first be recognized and then abandoned. This is what transcendence means to you from now on: it is the means by which you observe what you are experiencing within and decide what to keep and what to release. Love knows perfectly what feels comfortable and what does not. The heart knows the truth.

Extending joy cannot be something that involves effort. It cannot cost you anything to be the one you really are. Thus giving joy is the natural result of the release of guilt and does not require any kind of action or effort. I am asking you to stop looking for happiness and to begin to be happy because of the holiness that you are.

If you continue to respond on the basis of old thinking patterns, you will continue to create ideas about how things should be, and define in advance how you should be to be worthy.

This creates an ideal self that would bid you to go in search of it. This will never work.

What will work is for you to live in the truth of who you really are and not in illusion. Remind yourself as much as necessary that joy does not come from anything outside of you, because there is nothing outside of you. Recognize that if you are angry it is because in some way there is something that you do not like. You will know what you have judged as undesirable. Once you recognize what it is, then you can decide from love what to do or stop doing concerning it. You will begin to let go of the fear of feeling unhappy. Then you will begin to let go of the fear of fear.

Joy is a union with holiness; unhappiness, with fear. If we make this connection we can see more clearly how things work. Joy is the fruit of love; unhappiness the result of fear.

All fear has its origin in the fear of not being. Thus the opposite of joy arises from a fear of not being who you are. This is as true as the fact that the sun shines and blesses you with its light. Lack of joy is lack of love. A being cannot inhabit a place where there is no love.

We are understanding spiritual practices in a new way. We are inviting you to make truth so habitual that it finally becomes natural, something that you no longer need to think about, just as children do not think about what they are or how they should be. They just are what they are. They do not judge. They do not examine.

Joy is the fruit of love. Therefore recognize where sweetness dwells. By their fruits you will know them, as I said a while ago. I repeat it again. Where love is, there is the joy of being because being and love are one and the same. Christ is the joy of your being because that is the joy of the Mother. You who are Her beloved child cannot be anything other than the joy of God because Christ and your being are in an eternal union. They are the only reality.

I exhort you with pure love to go into the world telling happy stories, awakening true joy in the hearts of others, in the many ways you know how. There are plenty of reasons to praise and bless. There are many reasons to be happy, because Christ has come. Christ is here. And where He is, there always is love.

11.

I Have Known You Forever

A message from the Blessed Mother Mary

I. Prelude

Beloved child, observe how your soul grieves when you do not meet us, how much joy is lost when you wander through a world without meaning. And how much happiness you experience when you remain in the arms of your mother, wrapped in the warmth of my Immaculate Heart.

Holy child, you emerged from the heart of God and this loving mother, and there is no equal. The restlessness that springs in your heart when you are away from me is a holy feeling and a grace from Heaven. It helps you to be aware of how important these dialogues are. It reminds you of what comforts your being.

Feel the sadness of the soul when it is not with God. Recognize your joy when returning to the Mother's house. My heart is a safe haven for your mind, a perfect balm for your wounds. Its grace can cure all sickness. Whoever comes to me is never unsatisfied nor ever feels helpless in a world without holy love.

I am the source of the sweetness of love. I am the spring from where the pure waters of Christ flow. I am Mary, your mother and your being. My heart is the abode of eternal bliss.

Today I come to rescue you from the waters of oblivion. I have come to restore the holy communication that exists between you and me and between your being and God. We are a unit. We are the union of the three hearts made holy humanity.

Sometimes, as part of God's grace, you need to experience aridity of the heart. Although now you experience it in a new way, this feeling of not being connected with Christ serves to fix in your memory what makes you truly happy. It is a perfect means to remember that only love can make you happy. And that only in love can you be who you really are. This is why, again and again, we speak of love—we speak of you.

What else can I converse with you about but you, when you are my sleeplessness, my joy, and my being? As mother of the living, I have eyes only for my children. Child of my Immaculate Heart, nothing is important to God except Her beloved children. Just as my being would be torn apart if you separated from me, so is your soul able to receive the echo of that pain of separation. Never separate from your mother. Never separate from love. If you do, you will feel the cold of indifference.

There is no love other than the love of God. Thus I say that love is God and nothing but God. Your soul was created to live eternally in the joy of Heaven, in the joy of the Creator which is within your being of infinite love where you are safe and sound, forever cheerful in the certainty of being. Outside of God there is nothing. Within Her is everything, all created freely by Her holiness and mercy.

I have come to take you to dwell again within the circle of infinite love that extends from God the Mother to the Son and the Holy Spirit. You are not alone. You never were and never will be. When you feel that this mother has been somehow absent from your soul, remember that would be impossible, yet accept that sometimes it is necessary for you to experience the feeling of separation.

The memory of separation is deeply rooted in the human mind. I come to liberate you from that memory. That liberation is what this work in its entirety is about—to be free of the emotional memory that fear has caused in your mind and heart. Remember that when you created the unique consciousness that allowed fear to be perceived and to enter your mind and heart, it generated an outburst in your soul that stunned your mind and caused your heart to ache.

Do not be afraid to experience aridity of the heart; it will allow you now to remember your strong yearning for God. Remember that the awakening of that holy yearning will bring you to the truth that dwells within you.

The purification of the soul is a grace given by God. Nothing can happen in divine creation outside of the mind of the Creator. God knew that you could choose the path of fear, trying to create Her differently. God also knew before you were created the effects of the illusion that fear causes. She knew what was necessary to make Her children return home in due time, without limiting their freedom. God knows everything, because all is thought, feeling, and material and immaterial reality. God is everything of everything.

II. Purification

Within the pure potentiality of being, there is always and forever the possibility because of free will of denying reality. Its effect inevitably is projection—a desired reality alien to truth. However, along with that, God in Her infinite wisdom also created whatever was necessary to return to truth. This is the same as we have previously said, that your Mother and Creator not only gave you existence but also endowed you with whatever was necessary to sustain you within reality, so that you are safe and healthy even when you create realities that make you sick and alien to God.

Perfect love is the medicine for your soul as well as the source of your creation. The love of God can heal anything. This is why my Immaculate Heart is the source of your healing, because in it is only Divine Love.

Not infrequently the body experiences trauma, and yet you get closer to Heaven. These physical "events" which can manifest in multiple ways are clear evidence of blessed changes that occur within you.

The energy of God's love, if given in its totality without regulating its intensity, would cause the mind, the soul, and even the body to disintegrate. You could not bear so much love. This is the underlying reason for the feeling of being in a spiritual desert.

Often those who already savor the delights of God experience what is perceived as a departure from eternal love. If this were not so it would be detrimental to the soul. God knows when to give and when to take away, how to give and how not to give. There is a harmony in the flow of life. Giving and receiving must move at a pace that forms a melody of grace and holiness. Within the purity of the Creator is the rhythm of life, that which makes everything perfectly paced.

I have said that purification is necessary. This acts not only on your senses but on your beliefs. If what the body's senses show and what your beliefs tell are not revealed truth, then both dimensions of perception must be transformed. This transformation is not always easy, and in fact virtually never is.

Unlocking a false self to allow the true I, the Christ, to shine in all its glory is something of such magnitude that it is only possible thanks to the miraculous capacity of love, which is linked to infinite mercy. Nobody can do that except God.

Only the creator of souls knows each one in its totality. This is why, although there are many tools that are undoubtedly very valuable and beneficial for my children, none of them is essential. The essential is the revealed truth because only from the mind of God can you know what you really are. And if you do not know yourself, you will not leave the dual state of consciousness, which is the central problem of your existence. I say "your existence" because there are other creative dimensions beyond space and time, and in them are other challenges.

Not infrequently you have to confront nothingness, even while being everything in God. This situation need not become a battle. Simply go through it with trust. Doing so will make it possible to travel through life in peace, with greater confidence, and greater serenity. The more serenity, the more joy.

There isn't a single feeling in you, nor a single thought, that does not come from Christ. This must be reiterated until you feel comfortable with it and have recognized the Christ being as your true being, in perfect harmony with the will of your Heavenly Mother. Trust your being. Trust your soul's process. Trust everything that you experience.

Be afraid of nothing, even those states that are sometimes called a creative block or a momentary loss of inspiration. They are simply that, momentary. In being, nothing is lost. Consciousness cannot go back but always advances.

Sometimes it seems difficult to discern between reality and fiction, between truth and illusion. This difficulty will persist for a while, and then disappear. Have patience with yourself, blessed soul of our Mother.

The wall that used to demarcate a limit that separated Heaven from Earth is beginning to disappear, little by little. It is no longer as clear and immovable as it once was. That old wall is now but a bit of straw, as easily removed as for the wind to blow a leaf in autumn. Now you can unite the human and the divine, understanding that love is the source of every being, and that everything in the material world is either a manifestation of love or of a lack of love.

You are now in a perfect condition to accept that there is nothing external to you. Therefore, there is no longer any need for concern or fear of what you used to call the outside world. The belief that anything outside of you is real can no longer precipitate panic. Who would not fear such an impersonal universe, if it were perceived as something alien?

What is not part of you never was created and is not real. This is the basis of your fear of the world. When you consider something alien to yourself, you fear it because you cannot understand it. All true knowledge is knowledge of yourself. You need no other kind of knowledge except what God reveals to you about your being.

You need not know the laws of nature or the universe. When you try to understand them, even as humanity, you fall into a trap: the trap of believing that what you are seeking to know is the essence of things, when in fact you are seeking to govern life, to master it. To believe that knowledge is a method of control in order to be more secure is to believe in manipulation as a means of protection. God does not manipulate. You need not either.

Manipulation is one of the oldest schemes of the ego. Even children do it. In fact, babies know how to manipulate. The attempt to manipulate truth is equivalent to the desire to create without God—to transform divine creation into what you would like it to be, rather than love it as it really is. Remember, the problem of separation originates in the belief that you can change creation, that you want to do it, and that you have. This cannot but breed fear because if you could change reality, you could eliminate it, including yourself.

Child of Heaven, you cannot change what is real. You cannot change the holiness that you truly are. You cannot adulterate anything, because reality cannot be modified. Herein lies the peace of God.

III. Loving Love

I f Heaven and Earth are one, then human and divine reality have to be one. If this is true, and I assure you that it is, then you cannot escape the challenges of the world by thinking that since you belong to Heaven, you should not get involved in ordinary life. It is on Earth that you begin to live your Heaven and where you show others the God you truly are. This means that solidarity of love is essential to the soul.

If love were not in solidarity, God would not be so directly involved in your salvation. Every problem of the child is the problem of the Heavenly Mother. She takes on the affairs of every soul at every level, as a matter of honor.

For those who hunger, God is a plate of rice because that rice represents the possibility of being alive and God is the source of life. For those who do not have shelter, a home is God, because God is one's safe refuge and souls know it. What I am trying to say is not to disregard the issues of life, of what your brothers and sisters experience.

To think that the problems of your sisters and brothers do not concern you is not to believe in unity. Unity does not have to create a weight of worries or efforts to change a world in ways that seems futile. The world must change. And it will.

Creating a new world is a higher way to change the world. By saying this I wish not to create divisions but to make clear the difference that exists between modifying a system and replacing it anew. Creating "a new world" is an expression indicating that the systems that govern the world cannot be lastingly modified because their foundations are inharmonious with love and truth.

Fixing the world, as if it were a matter of repairing a deteriorated house or mending a tunic, is what humans have been trying to do over and over again. Sometimes the patches seem to fix things, but they always generate disharmony and finally do not work in a lasting way. You are not called to patch up the life you know but to replace it with eternal life.

Surely the ego can show solidarity and often does. But it is also true that love is solidarity; otherwise the ego would never have disguised itself as solidarity. Remember, the ego is the great imitator of God—emulated and simultaneously distorted.

To feed the hungry or give a drink to the thirsty in the name of love means that every act of charity must be born from a dialogue with your true being, the living Christ who lives in you, from that place where contemplation, meditation, or whatever comes from within must emerge. You can do a lot of good even while self-centered, but you will not be extending the love that you truly are. That need not be the case. You can make solidarity with love a living expression of love in action; in fact, love will always claim that union.

A love that cannot include material reality is a limited love and therefore cannot be the love of God. The Creator of the holy, beautiful, and perfect cannot be excluded from a reality according to your wishes. If you could live where it would be impossible for God to enter, you would be in a dimension outside of creation. That is impossible. I assure you that even in that place called hell, Christ can make an appearance if your heart allows it.

Love has no limits. Therefore, there is no reason for any aspect of your life to be excluded from its healing, restorative, and salvific power. To believe that the world cannot be transformed by the love of God is absurd, since love is infinite. You may accept this mentally, but acceptance in the mind alone does not achieve unity of being. It is necessary for this truth be experienced, so that the heart and mind are absorbed in it.

The salvific aspect of love is often overlooked. You must carry this in your awareness. Although the plan of salvation was not devised by you or by your sisters and brothers but by the One who created the universe, it is also true that God does nothing in an exclusive way. God is perfect inclusion because love is that.

Salvation is typical of love, as are so many other dimensions of love. If God, who is love and nothing but love, has a salvific aspect, you must also have it because you were created in Her likeness. That you do not connect with that aspect of being does not mean it does not exist.

You can and must save the world if you are going to live in the truth of your being. Everyone is called to do so. There is nothing unusual about this. Wouldn't a tender mother or a loving father do everything in their power to save their child from anything? If this feeling exists in the human heart, it must also exist in God.

The heart of every woman and every man is a perfect reflection of the Sacred Heart of Jesus and of my Immaculate Heart, for nothing in human nature is separate from spirit. Even the body is in union with the soul, its being, and its source.

Because the body and everything that you are is in union with spirit, the salvific aspect of love cannot exclude anything that constitutes the experience of human life. Remember, to God everything about you is important.

To save is to heal. To heal is to make happy. To make happy is to live in the fullness of being. So body, mind, and spirit must be in harmony to live in peace. This harmony is reached when there is unity between the purpose of mind, heart, and spirit or being. Undoubtedly, if the mind goes to one side, the heart to the other, and the being to another, your inner self is bewildered. Once more I speak of living in integrity with all that you are.

Do not think of salvation as necessary because you are a miserable sinner or unworthy. Understand it simply for what it is: the restoration of harmony in all that you are and wish to be.

If tomorrow you were told that scientists had found a pill that eliminates every disease and every problem in your life, before taking it would you spend years trying to understand how that would be possible or how it would work? Or would you simply determine whether the person telling you is trustworthy, and if so, take the medicine?

That is how it is with salvation. You know that only love will save the world, and love will do so because of what it is: salvific love. Therefore, you need not be concerned about how love will manage to replace a world without love with one whose foundation is truth. It will be done because it is God's promise. My child, peace will be attained. This is more certain than the path of the sun each day, or that rain falls, waters the grass, and then return to the sky.

The peace of God will reign in the world because the Creator has ordained it. This will be achieved not only through God but through unity among all men and women, and between them and their Creator. Do not leave everything in the hands of God alone, nor in the hands of humankind alone, for creation is an act of union, an extension of holy communion. We are one mind, one holy love.

IV. The Abode of Heaven

It has been said that in Heaven there are many mansions and that the whole is the Kingdom. This means that each mansion is something like a face of the love of infinite faces. Certainly, the whole cannot have divisions. Therefore, what the mansions of Heaven represent are different aspects of pure love. Since your soul is the likeness of its Creator, then in your soul all the mansions of Heaven must exist, all forms of the expression of love.

Love has infinite aspects or dimensions. It is present love and also inclusive love. It is love that teaches and also saves. It is love that corrects and also illumines. It is love that creates new love, love that renews the face of the Earth and everything that exists.

The salvific capacity of love and the ability to make all things new are the same. Therefore, it is necessary that the feelings of solidarity in your heart be manifested as a living expression of a love binding you and your brother and sister as a unit.

Trying to improve a world like the one you have been seeing is an endeavor that belongs to love. Remember, when the ego interfered you perceived a contradiction in your mind and heart between what your egoic thinking proposed as salvation and what the Holy Spirit knows is always true. One believes that improvement comes from the individual action of a person, a group, or of all humanity collectively. In other words, God is not needed. The other knows that this is impossible, because salvation comes from the love that God is and manifests in humanity as a whole, in unity with its source. The ego cannot know what salvation is because the ego is ignorant. Love knows because it is the wisdom of God.

Humanity, united with one another and with God, will cause a new Heaven and a new Earth to arise because in that union resides the peace of the Kingdom. And only from lasting peace can a peaceful world be created in which love can reign without limit.

Another reason why true charity can only be expressed through union with Christ is because only it can know what is best for a soul in the totality of every time, place, and circumstance. Being in union with Christ, each soul is affected in some way by each aspect of creation, and the totality of the universe as well. To interconnect all these relationships for each action, feeling, and thought is proper to Christ because it is the totality of love.

To find solutions to the problems of the world by leaving Divine Love aside is the way of separation. That cannot be a true solution because separation is the basic problem. Any system of thought that does not include the totality, the human and the divine, putting them on the same footing, perpetuates division and lack. Living as if you were just a body is living in separation, as much an error as living as if you were just spirit.

Equanimity leads to harmony. The balance between the Earthly and the Heavenly must be recovered for peace to reign in hearts. You restore that balance every time you seek unity with the being that you truly are because when you dwell in the abode of truth, you cannot deny your humanity, your Christ self, or the union you are with all creation.

Living in the unity of being by staying united to my Immaculate Heart, in union with the Sacred Heart of Jesus, is how you reside in the abode of Christ. You allow Christ consciousness to inform you of the action or inaction required. Once informed, the being will do or refrain from doing whatever love inspires. This leads to the true solution because everything done from that union cancels separation and its effects.

Again and again, I ask you not to separate yourself from my Immaculate Love because in holy love you reach the fullness of being and create a new Heaven and a new Earth. This is how divisions disappear and how you become aware of the union that everything is.

It is from the peace of the soul that you will create the new world. In that peace you are one with your sisters and brothers and with God. This is how you call upon love and invite it to be part of your relationships with everyone. This is how you help your brothers and sisters out of their dark cells of ignorance and the desolate corners of separation. You save the world by being the peace of Christ.

Brother of Christ and of everything created! Sister of light! You are not called to strive, nor to change the world, but to allow the old illusory reality to be replaced in all its dimensions, in you and the whole universe—not amending things, but creating the new based on the love you truly are—replacing what is not real, because it was never created, with what it is, which comes from God. Discord is abandoned. Harmony reigns.

The only way for you to live in the reality of love—and thereby allow everyone to live in it because of the unity you are with everyone and everything—is returning to and remaining in a direct relationship with God. From this relationship the miracle of creation unfolds before you and through you. It is from your relationship with Christ that you create a new love, because Christ is that unity. And from that unity you abolish separation now and forever, from the love that you truly are, from where Heaven touches Earth. It is in your direct relationship with God that the greatest effect you could ever imagine is produced.

Child of holiness, remain always in unity with God and you will be living in the Kingdom of Heaven. Your sisters and brothers need you. They, more than anyone, are calling you from every corner of the world telling you: Beloved brother, dear sister, let us dwell together in the Heaven of direct relationship with God now and forever. Let us live united in the concord of Mary, mother of the living. Together we will sing a new song. We will live forever in the mansion of light. We will be one forever and will shine in the presence of love.

12.

The Divinity
of the Soul

A message from the Blessed Mother Mary

I. Prelude

Beloved soul in love with Christ, child of a God who is infinite love, today I make an appearance united with a choir of angels of God and the beings of light that illuminate creation with their beauty and goodness. I am the eternal maiden of God. I am the always pure. I have come in response to your call and in union with the will of the Mother of Lights. I am the mother of everything and everyone. I am the unity of love. I have come to gather, not to criticize. I am here for pure love. I meet with my children in all possible ways according to their disposition and nature.

Everyone has a way of being. I communicate with souls in the way each one can and desires. I do not deny my voice as the mother of Christ. You all need a mother. This is as true in the plane of physical bodies as in the life of the spirit. The mother is the one who nurtures, protects, and, above all, covers the child with love. I come also for the relationship between the soul and its source.

I am the source of life. I am the rain descended from Heaven that has come to water the Earth and everything that exists in it with a love that has neither beginning nor end. I am a purity that cannot be stained, holiness that cannot be desecrated, an inviolate love from whence all of Heaven extends to all and everything.

I have come to remind you all of the divinity of your soul. This truth you already know but often leave aside when submerged in the apparent problems of life. Do not be fooled by the mental pattern that would trap you in endless dilemmas that have no solution, for they are not real.

Receive these words and share with the world. I also speak to all those who are part of God's plan for this blessed work which arises from the heart of God and to all who wish to hear my voice. I speak to you with all my heart. Remember that being is a holy union that remains one with everything, so that the communion of your hearts and minds allows the voice of truth to shine in souls in unison. It shines for everyone. Some see that flash and follow it like a star. Others do not.

Not everyone stops to contemplate the sun each morning, or the beauty of starry nights, even though both are holy creations. The same is true of the truth that shines in all minds and the holy love that calls all hearts.

It is necessary to remember the divinity of the soul and its ineffable beauty; otherwise, the mind tends to consider itself as a being of no consciousness, a reality disconnected from the source of life. In doing so it annuls its spiritual reality, from where it is nourished in order to be what it is. The mind of God is the source of your mind. The soul is endowed with reason to live united to divine truth. It was also endowed with free will because there can be no love without freedom. Everyone is free to think about one thing or another, but no one is free to establish what is true.

Free will makes you similar to God because it is the same as love. Remember, love is freedom. This is why God will never transgress your freedom. You can always remain united to me in body and soul by giving me your thoughts, feelings, and will, or not. That you do one thing or another will not change the love I feel for you or the love of all Heaven for a holy child of God. You will always be a child of light, even if you decide not to shine.

II. The Mystery of Your Being

You were created in a perfect act of love reflecting a beauty that surpasses all measure. You are indeed the pure extension of the beauty of Christ. The colors of your soul shine increasingly as we proceed together on the path of love. I say "the path of love" because you have already completed the path of the heart, which leads to the path of transformation, and from it to the path of knowledge, as has already been revealed.

The world needs to recover the mystical dimension of its existence, a dimension that was lost little by little, giving way to an intellect not anchored in truth and a heart far from love. This return to the source of love is a return to the holy relationship that joins you with your Creator along with every living being.

Everyone will return to love because it is the will of God. This does not mean that everyone agrees to live eternally in the Mother's house, but that love will shine in all its glory in each created mind and will be recognized for what it is. Some will joyfully sing a welcome song. Others will look at it as if it were a beautiful but meaningless sunset, and will continue their ways without stopping to contemplate the wonders that God created. Even so, they are still children of love, saints because of their source and perfect because of what they are. Everything is perfect in God's creation.

You are being invited again and again to choose only love and nothing but love. This is the choice all are called to make. It is the choice of Adam and Eve, your choice, and that of your sisters and brothers. This decision must be made in every moment. In it you renew your existence. Every time you say "yes" to love, all the creative force of God, which gave birth to your soul and the whole universe, explodes into a creative act without equal and makes you something new.

Getting stuck in senses and desires is to live a limited reality apart from the eternal reality of love. This does not mean that you loathe your senses or the sensations they seem to create. It simply means what it says. There is no need to deny the body or its senses, nor the desires of the heart. All this has led you to salvation, that is, it has already taken you to the heaven of your holy mind.

You can never limit the power of God. In this fact lies the certainty of your eternal permanence and the sanctity of your being. To join God is to unite with what is real in you, because you unite to what is similar to your being. Within that union, your reality of infinite love is created and recreated in a constant flow of divine giving and receiving. In this relationship God unites with you and you become one with God.

Choosing only love is to make the fundamental choice that the soul is called upon to make. Living on Earth within that is the call being made from above to humanity, in these last times.

III. Christ on Earth

My heart is calling you. Love is calling everyone regardless of their origin. Remember, the heart does not care where love comes from as long as it comes. To let oneself be carried away body and soul by the love of God in perfect freedom is to allow the divine to emerge from the mystery of life and constantly spill over you to the world, sowing love. The world will begin to see you no more with the eyes of the body and you will continue to enlighten souls from the spiritual reality of the Kingdom. Living within the limits of time cannot prevent living in the love that God is, because the soul is not subject to time or space. The pure soul is unlimited. It is not anywhere. It dwells only in the heart of God.

In your heart lies the wisdom of God. Nothing can change that because the only reality is love and love never changes, nor does its wisdom. Wherever you go your soul accompanies you. What you are will always accompany you. Consequently your mind cannot cease to live in sanctity, even if for a time it prefers to forget about God.

The deepest aspiration of the soul is to live always in union with the truth of its being—in unity with the will of the Creator. When both wills merge, then the soul and the Creator are united. It is this unity that we call a holy relationship. In it your being imbibes your humanity and expresses your divinity. It takes no effort at all. No technique can teach it. You know how to do it perfectly because it is part of you.

To live on Earth as the divine being that you are is possible and the only way to live from now on. There is no going back. This is why you are invited to return to your mystical dimension regardless of how you express yourself. Form, regardless of whether physical or spiritual, is the means of expression—means, not ends. All have the purpose of expressing the unknown.

Only through forms are beings expressed. You are one of them, as beautiful and holy as any form that comes from love. Having your divine form manifest on Earth is ultimately the reason you have come into the world. Here and now you begin to be the divinity of which God made you. This you will do also in the realm of no time, since God's purpose for you is to make yourself known to Her in all your beauty, splendor, magnificence, and sanctity.

IV. The Doubt of the Prophet

Now it is necessary to be aware of what I call the doubt of the prophet. It is a state in which the mind is absorbed by thoughts of the past, namely that you are incapable of representing divinity with your humanity. That thought pattern must be set aside. It is an old way of thinking.

You know that you have received a mission from Heaven. You know that you receive thoughts that you do not think. You know very well the nature of those incomparable thoughts that come to you with authority. You know this with certainty. But you do not know what to do.

This not knowing what to do with the revelation you receive arises simply from doubt about yourself. It is impossible for you not to be provided with the necessary means to express your divinity in the world of time and space. Remember, all doubt is doubt about yourself.

Once you open the doors to revealed truth, you begin to walk on Earth as the living Christ, a way of being completely different from any way of being in the world. This difference causes you go through a time in which you know not how to live with the truth at your side. The tension between the truth that you are—

and that you have joyfully recognized in the depths of your mind and heart—and the mental confrontation of continuing to live in a world of apparent limitations governed by a thought system so alien to what you have seen and heard, is something you must recognize and transcend.

You are united with Christ. Thoughts you "did not think" came to you with an unparalleled authority, certainty, and agility. They are your true thoughts. Recognizing this is essential to continuing peacefully along the path of truth. You are truth revealed to yourself from Heaven. There is no such thing as a truth over there and you over here. The sacred revelation that comes to you is the revelation of your true divine being to your true human being. It is not an external something being revealed. It is God revealing Herself.

For so long you have conceived of God, the Supreme Being, the Truth, or even perfect Love as something apart from you. Now I must disidentify your mind with any idea of separation that may still exist. It is what every prophet must go through.

There is no one in the world who, by hearing the voice of God, does not pass through this. We call it the doubt of the prophet, a doubt that presents itself in a thousand ways. It might present itself as a persistent idea that tells you that you will not succeed in what you know you should do. It might present itself in the form of believing that God will abandon you to your fate. Sometimes this doubt manifests itself as a sense of disconnection from your mission. It might present itself as a desire to drop everything under the false premise that your contribution to the truth is futile, less than a grain of sand in the middle a desert, that you have no impact or reason for being.

While the temptations of doubt may appear, and frequently do, yet observe that something tells you that you know for certain that you will not abdicate. There is no turning back. You know you have made a fundamental, irrevocable choice. You have decided with all your soul, mind, and heart to live through the truth that has been revealed.

To live in your truth is to live the love that you are. You know this. You also know the veracity of what is being given to you here. You know in the depths of your heart that the words that come through this work come from a truth that is always true. You also know that this truth is what you are. What you still do not know is how to feel completely comfortable with who you really are. This is because in the past you have not felt comfortable with who you were. A separated self could not feel comfortable with itself.

Begin to be aware of your relationship with truth. There is no real distance between the living Christ who lives in you and the Christ of God who is part of divine essence. You are Christ, in the sense that both are of the same mind.

You have come to know the truth of yourself. The truth has been revealed. You know that this channel of direct communication between your mind and the divine mind has been opened and will never close. Knowing this is one thing, but knowing how to relate to it is a very different matter. Thus the prophet's doubt is really an echo of a way of thinking, a pattern of thought and emotional response that comes from the old being you once thought you were.

To believe yourself as an unworthy child of God or incapable of taking care of your Mother's affairs has been the funereal song you have heard over and again. Doubt will disappear forever when you cease to hear that dark melody and listen to the symphony of the Heaven of your holy mind.

The truth is revealed to you so as to produce real effects on your life and the world. When truth reaches the human aspect of your being, it also creates the necessary conditions for it to manifest itself in form. Living as Christ is possible, and in fact is the most natural thing in the world; there is no risk of failure.

Another thing to be mindful of about the prophet's doubt is the fear of falling. That fear, too, comes from the lack of certainty of yourself. You cannot fall because Christ does not fall. You cannot be wrong because what is united to God forms a union with Her and God is not mistaken. It is impossible not to be given the means to be who you are. They will be given to you abundantly, in a measure beyond your imagination. God satisfies your needs above and beyond what you are capable of desiring.

You need not carry saddlebags on this path, nor a tunic just in case. Everything will be provided, both material and spiritual. Everything that the work of expressing the truth requires will be given. Everything. Otherwise, the plan of love for you and the whole world would be incomplete and impossible. Once God is revealed to you, once the truth about you is shown, your mind changes its purpose. This change of purpose is sometimes experienced as difficult.

The relationship between who you are and yourself is your first relationship, indeed the only one that exists for you. This means that how you treat yourself, how you love yourself, how you respond to what you are, is how you will relate to everything and everyone. Said another way, as you relate to God you will relate to yourself, your sisters and brothers, and the universe.

It may not be comfortable or easy at first to become accustomed to living in a way so different from how you used to live. But the discomfort will be temporary. Everything changes when love makes an appearance in your life and establishes a perpetual relationship with you based on truth and holiness. Didn't everything change when my divine son Jesus brought love to the world?

The power of love is beyond all human understanding. Its force cannot be overestimated. Its strength creates everything necessary for the expression of the truth of who you are. Remember, love has the power to create new love. Thus, the means for what has been revealed to you can be manifested in your human reality, created by reason of the relationship you established.

All doubt is doubt about the capacity of your being to be the one it is in truth. The thinking mind, so accustomed to thinking in a conditional way, cannot understand the reality of the unity that you are with God. That part of the mind does not know the new. It is scared when mystery presents itself. Novelty cannot be digested by a mind that always seeks assurances from that which is untrue.

The thinking mind, or old conditioned mental patterns, cannot embrace mystery because mystery cannot pass through the filter of linear reasoning. You are unlimited, which linearity cannot encompass.

The Divine Mind is multi-dimensional, just as love is and you are. Linear thinking insists upon "if this, then that," which is "normal" to its way of thinking. Mentality that does not adhere to that logic is considered insane, although the opposite is true.

Another doubt of the prophet, then, is the fear of madness. It often presents itself to the prophet as the fear of letting go of a thought pattern deeply rooted in survival, the foundation of the world. The conditioned mind is challenged by the new miracle-mindedness, the mind of Christ or unconditioned mind. Although you are already well entrenched in the real or Divine Mind, and you know that you live in it, old thought patterns still arise and tell you that this is impossible, that you cannot survive with this new mentality.

One of the clearest manifestations of thinking apart from the truth is the relationship between money and spirituality. I will now consider this aspect.

V. New Being, New Life

Not to have enough is a base fear. Many are lost in it. Even among those who sincerely have embraced the truth it is common to experience the conflict between the human and the divine in this aspect of life. In fact, it is often a major obstacle. God does not call you and then leave you desolate, yet you must answer the call, and you know that God constantly cares and assists with the sustenance of life.

Ultimately, all fear comes from doubt, and all doubt comes from a lack of certainty, a lack of confidence, about yourself. Trust is essential for the prophet; and trust is often put to the test with respect to money.

You know what you really are. It has been revealed. You know that your sister and brother are the same, regardless of whether or not they recognize it. You must now take that very high consciousness and live it. This means relating to yourself as well as your sisters and brothers as holy children of God, not out of belief, but out of revealed truth.

As you increasingly join with those who, like you, have made the fundamental choice for love, you will consolidate in your mind the reality of what you are. Being a new being is at first not easy, even if it be the deepest longing of your soul. This apparent difficulty will cease when you realize that who you were previously was not real. It required you to feed it constantly, and strive to "be that" which you thought you were supposed to be. True being does not require vigilance, effort, dedication, or anything. Quite the opposite.

Effort is of the ego. Sustaining such an identity requires dedication and energy. It is as if you were trying to sustain a corpse that in each moment collapses due to its inherent lack of life. Such effort has worn on your soul. You may still believe—but not for much longer—that the divine being that you truly are, the Christ in you, also requires vigilance and effort. Nothing could be further from the truth.

What you really are comes from God. It will never cease to be. Look at the world. Do not judge anything, just look for one or two minutes. Then consider the following: to try to hide your true self you had to create the world that your eyes see, so vast and immense. Even so, you could never obliterate your true self.

The totality of the physical universe and the entire history of humankind, with so many twists and turns, has not made a dent in your divinity. The world as a whole is to Christ as less than a grain of sand to all the planets combined. As one with the being that God is, your being holds in the palm of your hand the entire universe as you would hold a nut in your hand.

Do not fail to recognize and bring often to consciousness the divine dimension of your soul, or you run the risk of denying that part of yourself from which everything true arises. If you deny the Christ in you, you deny the totality of yourself. If you accept that you are the abode of Christ and that everything that Christ is resides in you, you accept your magnificence.

Perhaps you think that this matter of recognizing the divinity and eternality of your soul has no relationship with your daily life. The mind may say: "God may live in me but still I have to pay the bills and deal with situations so earthly that it seems impossible to believe in this matter of my divinity— maybe it will be true when I leave the world."

That type of thought, very much ingrained in the separate mind, is typical of egoic thinking. It arises from the belief in the reality of the body. Yet the body is not real, much less an end. That does not mean that it does not exist—do not confuse levels. The body is the means by which the human physical dimension is experienced. Simply that. It is a system endowed with senses that allow you to interact with physical reality. It comes into time and disappears in time as does everything that arises in it.

Beloved child, I am here, united with your divinity, submerged in the unfathomable depths of the Mother's love. I come wrapped in Divine Grace to take you to great depths of the mystery of love, which is the mystery of your being.

You were created by infinite love to be infinitely loved. You were created to live eternally in the endless bliss that is God. With joy and gratitude that I remain with you, in you. Through our union we express, in this work, the love of God in a particular way. You are the joy of the mother of the living and of all creation. You are mystery. You are life. You are bliss.

My holiness remains united to your holiness because we are one in God. We live, beloved child, in the Mother's house wherein dwells the sweetness of love. We are a holy unit. In Christ we are one mind, one holy heart, one soul, one single being united in my Immaculate Heart, which remains united to the Sacred Heart of my divine son Jesus. We are the fullness of being.

I have come in all your glory and splendor, wrapped in your beauty that comes from the creator of the holy, the perfect, the beautiful. Together we are the beauty of Heaven. We are the pure of heart. We are saints. We are united. These words are not spoken by a being external to you. I, by the will of the Mother and your own will, echo and use a voice that is yours, mine, and the voice of the God of all that is true.

"Love" is a living and life-giving word. Love is the voice of Christ and in every real voice. Love is the only source of every voice that speaks in spirit and in truth. Love is the foundation of life and reason. Love is what gives life to everything that lives eternally. Love is what allows the mind to think and the heart to extend. The word has been given to you to explore and join. In that eternal exploration, the soul remains forever in the ecstasy, contemplating its joy and fulfillment. There, in the eternal coming to know of the mystery of mysteries, is where the source of eternal life is found. Such coming to know is the sustenance of your being.

The knowledge of God has no end. It is infinite. You will never finish wondering about your unfathomable divine soul. You are divine. You are human. You are everything.

In this session you are invited to remember, once again, that the mystery of love never ends. It is a call to embrace the unfathomable reality of being. To recognize that the power of love cannot be overestimated. Such power exists. It is a driving force. It is the vital energy giving movement to everything. Remember, life is movement, an eternal flow of perpetual creation. The creative engine feeds on love and is love. It is such a powerful force that many have feared it. From this arose the fear of God.

All the strength of God's love lives in you. It is why often the body cannot easily withstand its power and its cells must adapt to the flow of divine union. It is why many physical alterations arise when you join with truth. It is the observable result of a transformation taking place in the mind, whose effect manifests in the body. It is part of God's plan, not something that should cause worry.

Because love makes all things new, allowing your humanity to be reunited with your divinity means the renewal of your humanity. Such novelty causes a period of discomfort. It is temporary. Ideally you will release your resistance and surrender once and for all to love. Let yourself be carried by love without trying to control anything. And don't worry: this response usually happens after a while, rarely at the beginning.

Surrender to love and you will begin to fly the flight of freedom in a way never before experienced, a flight that will take you and many others to unimaginable heights. You are ready. Just let everything be the way it is. Do not judge anything. Trust. Remember that there is a time for everything. Nothing happens to a child of God by chance. Everything is for a higher good.

My beloved, your life and all that you are is in the hands of love. Rest in the peace of your being. Remain there always. From peace you will create a new Heaven and a new Earth whose foundation is love. You will witness your work, because it is the will of God that everything be known.

13.

The Wound of God

A message from Jesus

I. Ecstasy and Joy of the Soul

Holy child of divine beauty! You seek ways to express in the world the truth you have seen and heard that is beyond all human words. Among a multitude of angels, my voice is present with you in this time of love and unity. I come for love. I speak for love. I do everything for love. "Love is what we are and everything we do" is an expression of our being of peace and truth.

When you remember that you are a being of pure light, as beautiful as the most spectacular sunset and even much, much more, and as vast as the universe but much more, you will begin to realize the abundance you have to give. You would like to give everything to everyone but that feels impossible. The conduit through which you express yourself seems incapable of so much overflowing energy. But you are the force of the universe made into humanity.

I cannot speak in any way other than as a faithful lover speaks to his beloved. All the love of creation resides in our angelic heart, united with the Mother of creation, with the living Christ, and with you. From us flows a love without beginning or end. Within our holy relationship dwells the eternal relationship

God has with you. In the center of that relationship of triune love—in which your being is radiant—dwells your reality, like a child in the mother's womb.

A direct relationship with God is the reality of perfect love. It is not a relationship like those you usually know in the world. In a divine relationship everything is of the truth, including your being. Everything is embraced in a divine relationship. Life is an expression of that relationship.

One of the essential aspects of your relationship with God is the admiration that celestial love arouses. When the soul begins to open itself to mystery and accepts union, it receives lights in its understanding. These give a special clarity, through which comes an extraordinary contemplation of divine mystery. Seeing beauty previously unimagined, the soul is admired. The soul immerses itself in an ecstasy of contemplation of the wonders of Divine Love. Now the soul only wants the things of Heaven. It just wants to live for love. It is captivated by a love without compare.

The admiration of pleasant things adheres strongly in the soul, both because of the excellence of the beauty seen, and because of its novelty. One never tires of seeing, and, seeing, experiencing great joy. Admiration and love go hand-in-hand.

We could say that God hurts the soul with inducements of softness, so that, like a needle attracted by a magnet, it turns and changes its trajectory towards the pole; whereupon the will, wounded by heavenly love, throws itself into Her arms and is taken to God and stripped of all inclinations not of Her. Thus the soul enters into rapture, not of knowledge, but of joy; not of admiration, but of affection; not of science, but of experience; not of seeing, but of tasting.

In a divine union, when the husband visits the beloved, he feels her soul to be wounded in a very exquisite way. Although he may not understand how she was hurt, he knows that what hurt her is something of great beauty and joy, something she would never want healed. In that delight of the soul with its God, the mind seeks to grasp the beloved, clinging to his being. Not being able to possess it as she would possess the things of the world, she suffers a pain so joyful that, even so, she prefers to be a thousand times wounded by the presence of her celestial lover.

The heart of the soul united with God is wounded by a love so exquisite it will never again enjoy anything that does not have the quality of Heaven. Since the heart clings to the greatest experience of joy it has, once it has enjoyed the juices of Divine Love it will not want to leave that place where it has experienced such delight. This ecstasy of love and contemplation is the joy of union—a taste as sweet and serene, as affable and safe as any can give to the soul.

The soul returns to the ecstasy of divine union where it is what it was called to be from its moment of creation. There it is as it was created to be. Joy and the irresistible desire to remain is the result of experiencing the unity of the soul. Within divine union lies the refuge of being. Everything that the heart seeks it finds in union with Divine Love. Once Christ kisses the soul, it will never look for anything other than that which it cannot say, but surely feels. Often the mind experiences difficulty translating that experience into words, causing internal tension, for now the soul is torn between dying of this longing for love and living united to its only love.

II. The Soul Knows God

The soul knows who created it, and will always return to its first love, God. This is what happens on the spiritual path. In reality it is a journey back to that which the heart knows is of incomparable beauty, delight, and joy. The soul that has known God in this world is disgusted because in spite of the raptures and ecstasies of contemplation which God has given, not being able to hold on to Her definitively makes it feel like an aftertaste, like a loving partner suffering the absence of their beloved spouse, or a child whose parent is on a long trip.

A soul united with God remains enamored of Her. It experiences small glimpses of divine delights. It is transformed by experiences of unity. With this transformation comes the reality of a new being, because love has the ability to unite everything with God. Only love can make that happen. Love unites the soul with its Creator. Each act of love for the deity, or rather every feeling felt from the depth of your being for God, increases or enlarges the heart to love more and more.

God enlarges your heart imperceptibly. The mind does not participate, nor the heart itself, but both become conscious of this widening once it has been realized. This is why souls pierced by the dart of Divine Love begin to recognize things that did not previously exist—expressions of love, sweetness, beauty, and holiness emerge that had not emerged before. This transformation by Divine Love in the soul, although its effects are not perceptible until afterwards, can leave the mind stunned for a while until mind and heart come together.

The memory of God is currently how you remain in the Mother's house. Although you cannot put it into words, you know that your desire to return to that state will guide you to the eternal abode of truth. You know something has happened, something sublime, not of the world. In short, Christ has kissed your soul and anointed your forehead with holy oil.

You are aware that something has happened, but now you debate between understanding what happened and deciding what to do with it, a debate that may last for a long while before you let it go. Divine Love has broken into your life as a result of your call united with your Mother's call. It is impossible for you to understand, such is the magnitude of change brought about in you and in everything.

I invite you to accept that you have had a mystical transformation that has changed your life completely and that there is no turning back. You have experienced divine union and must now take charge of your new state. You are not alone in this, of course, but it is something you must consciously assume. You are not who you were before and never can be again, nor would you want to go back. You are now the result of divine union with your being.

The unitive experience is so strong, so transformative, that even the body may often suffer. Everything changes when Christ kisses the soul. The deeper the union, the deeper the transformation. Remember, love has the ability to transmute everything, as well as to unite all that you are with God. Remember, love becomes one with the beloved.

The heart knows what love is. It needs no explanation. Trying to put into words what can never be articulated is foolish, although the world has been attempting to do so since Christ stepped on the Earth, and since God, through the human expression of the union of Mary and Jesus, reunited humanity with infinite love. Everything was then transformed to a degree that can never be understood. The same happens with you. When something joins with your being, it becomes holy love because of what you are.

The only difference that exists is your degree of union with God, with the whole—that is, what you join with and what you leave outside your being. Everything that is true and united in your consciousness makes you full. Everything you leave outside the scope of your consciousness forms a world of illusion, not because you really create something illusory but because only in illusion can you leave out truth.

You cannot separate yourself from truth. The truth is what you are. You cannot live in a state other than that of unity because, being one with God, you are unity.

The ecstasy of mystical union is not a union with anything external. It is the union of your whole being with itself. The effect of the state of union is joy and perfect peace. Sustaining that state of oneness is what the road to heaven is about.

You may have heard that the degree of union with Christ that you reach while you are in the world is not the same as that which you will attain when you are not in the body. That is not completely true, for there are no degrees of union. Union is total or not at all.

III. Divine Novelty

What differs between one union and another is your degree of awareness of it. In itself, mystical union contains the totality of the effects of God united with the soul. There are no degrees of holiness and no degrees of God. When you decided to join the love that created you, you decided to join with all the treasures of union, the totality of Divine Will. All the gifts of love were given to you at the moment of union.

The state of unity you have attained does not differ now from what will later be because with love there is no time and no such thing as before and after—only the reality of love. Everything else is illusory. Thus within your being already resides the qualities, inheritances, and goods of the Kingdom of Heaven in their totality; and they, by reason of their presence in your being, will realize what God Herself has entrusted to them. God does nothing in vain nor leaves his works unfinished.

You are the masterpiece of God's love. You cannot avoid being as complete as God Herself. I assure you that when you said "Yes" to Christ, you sealed a covenant of Divine Love that cannot be rescinded. The cause and effect of it will remain forever in the book of life of your eternal being.

The works of God cannot be understood as they happen. The most sensible attitude concerning what God does in you and through you is to have the attitude of silence, observance, and patience. It would be a waste of time to keep thinking about what happened and try to explain it. That would not cause harm, but it would delay your full joy. So I have come to you today to ask you to stop thinking about what happened and how new it is, and to accept the mystery of God's love and the promise that your union has made great things in you and will continue to do so forever.

The novelty of love is so great that the thinking mind can never decipher what happens when the embrace of Christ is consummated in your soul. You are the perfect result of the betrothal between your being and love—a generative union that has already given abundant fruit. Little by little you will see them and eternally create new realities of love. Mystical union fuses your soul with God. Leave everything you are in that new state. Novelty is admired by your being and is the joy of your soul.

Divine novelty brings joy and submerges your being in an ecstasy of love. The eternal novelty of love surpasses all imagination in beauty. The joy of the soul that sees God is of such magnitude that it faints in the arms of its Mother, and thus sleeps the holy sleep, a sleep not of forgetfulness, but of complete surrender to the love of loves.

Everything you are rests forever in the heart center of your Mother and Creator because you are one with Her. Just as you need do nothing because of your union with love, God becomes nothing in you when you and God are consummated. It takes not more than a moment of union for the new to emerge. Nothing remains the same as it was before Christ union. Some of these changes will be visible, but even those changes are minimal compared to the change your whole being.

Life acts silently and subtly. It does not boast. It does only what it must do, effectively and lovingly. The same goes for the wisdom of your being, which is the love of God. I say once again that the flow of divine union is a torrent of living water that flows from the source of eternal life and creates new life in you. This new life created within your being comes to light in due time, like the child inside a mother's womb. There is a time for everything. A time to fertilize, to grow, and to give birth. All those times are already part of who you are.

The phase of union, fertility, and conception contain within themselves what each of them requires as God conceived them to be. They are already in you. The only thing we wait upon together now is for each phase to be manifested in due time and, as God has already thought about it with you, united in the sanctity of being.

The phenomenon of mystical union is an event of the soul with such surprising effects that you cannot see them as they unfold. You can, however, know how you feel in yourself.

Once heavenly love has touched your heart, the whole world may try to persuade you that you have not had that experience. But you know you have. Nothing can make you doubt it. You also know how much you have changed and how much your life has changed. You know what you feel in your heart. Nothing and nobody can remove that perfect certainty.

We are speaking of the certainty of the heart, a certainty that comes from knowing what you feel, not from the thinking mind that expounds theories that can never be consistent because they do not arise from unshakable truth. Certainty cannot be explained but can be known, just as honey is sweeter and more tasty in your mouth than when it is swallowed. The same occurs with love. It grows as it is " ruffled," that is, as it is tasted in the heart and expressed, which it does in multiple ways. One of them is love's reception. Accepting the love that comes to you is the perfect answer to the heart's longing. And since God cannot be absent from you, the love that flows into your heart is permanent. Receiving Divine Love is what the soul desires constantly.

Letting yourself be loved and allowing your heart to expand to love without ceasing is what I ask of you. Love widens the heart to receive more love. Your being as a pure master grows more and more, so to speak, to encompass the totality of love. God wholly absorbs you when you let yourself love without measure.

Focus on receiving love. Let yourself be carried away by the sweetness of God. She has the control, the wisdom, and the gifts required for both you and your blessed work to unfold perfectly. Remember this so you do not confuse the work of love with concrete tasks, obligations, and activities. Remember that God is only interested in your being; nothing else is real.

IV. The Spark of the Soul

Being is what life is about. Being love is what the truth of you is about. Doing may or may not be necessary for expression of being. We recall this matter here so that you do not fall into the oblivion of thinking you are really only about being. That is the work of God.

Beloved of God! The beauty of your being, the holiness that comes from God and is expressed in you, the purity of your soul, will spread increasingly until you reach a point where that is all you see and you retain not even the slightest memory of what you are not and never were. The "I am" of the soul is the essence of being. It is what makes the soul exist. It is what gives life to being. It is the spirit of God in you.

Within the soul is a spark of life that we call the living spirit. That spark of love is the "I am." Without it, the soul would not exist—or if it were possible, it would exist as an empty entity, a nothing. What happens in the holy moment of divine union is that the "I am" which has been denied begins to be recognized again in freedom, affirming your choice for the divine will.

Once you recognize the "I am" of your soul, you begin to realize that being is the only important thing because it is the only essential thing. "To be or not to be" is the question the soul debates and on which God has placed all Her divinity. Not to be, if possible, would be the soul's tragedy. To be the "I am," that spark of divine light that lights the soul and sustains its existence, allows the fullness of a pure soul.

That spark of light that we here call the "I am" has been referred to as the "heart." In it resides all that God has eternally willed for you, Her beloved child. Within it is the foundation of eternal life, waiting for you to welcome it so it can shine with all its luminescence. This, in fact, is what you have done when you made the fundamental choice.

That spark of pure love is already shining like a radiant sun. You still cannot see the beautiful rays that flow from you and embrace everything, but you will, not with the eyes of the body but with those of Christ. You will see them with the eyes of love.

There is no possibility of failure in a life with God. We repeat this truth because it is necessary to do so. We do it for love. Likewise, there is no need for you to ask yourself how well we are doing, how God's work is going, or whether you are doing well or poorly. The work is not yours, even though done in you. The work is of the One who created us all with love.

When you joined Christ you captured Heaven for your soul—you united the divine with the human in the dimension that corresponds to your existence. I was the first to do that and I did it my way, two thousand years ago. My mother, who is also your mother, was also the first. It could be said that somehow we opened the door of departure so that you and your sisters and brothers in Christ can do their part in this work of collaboration that is salvation and the return to the house of love.

This work of word-symbols is part of God's great work. It was in the design before time began to roll. It is a living expression of the spark of light that you live. It is a particular extension of Divine Love, arising as a result of union with Christ. As others join in this holy manifestation, the spark of light that is your "I am" will grow more and more in its uniqueness as other "I ams" begin to express themselves in their unique ways. Thus this work will act as a catalyst for others to express what love is in their unique voice. Everyone is called to give a face to love.

The "I am" demands expression because that is implicit in its nature as the essence of being. Imagine a spark of light inside a holy soul. That spark carries within itself the laws of love. One of them is that of particular expression. To some extent the mission of this work is to awaken others to express themselves in their union with Christ in their unique way.

"Union with Christ" is synonymous with a direct relationship with God. In this sense, it is essential for this work that it be understood that the One who created us as saints has arranged that the golden rule of expression be the authenticity of the heart. That is why your heart does not rest in peace when it cannot be authentic.

God does not look for clones or a homogeneity that cancels diversity. Your "I am," joining increasingly with others "I am's," will illumine the world with a beauty that is beyond compare. From the sum of expressions of authentic love will emerge a world that can expand its capacity to give and receive love, just as the heart does.

In your capacity to love in freedom lies the world's liberation. In your union with Christ dwells the sweetness of love. In your direct relationship with God you create, in union with everything holy, beautiful, and perfect that which neither eye saw, nor ear heard, nor tongue uttered. Thus you extend, in unity, the wonders of God.

Remember, my child, you have the ability to make a whole Heaven. You are the child of God; as such the forces of creation unite with you to create new life, a life far from the plans the world has conceived. God's plans are so great as to be incomprehensible to the thinking mind. A conditional thinking system based on "if this, then that" would be like trying to put the vastness of the created universe in a tiny bottle.

The thoughts of God are beyond measure. Therefore, seek not to understand what happened to you when you joined the Christ in you—when God came to you and you let Her in. Trust the process. Trust your capacity to be in the flow. You have no idea what the heart of your Mother is like, united to yours in a union of perfect love. Allow Her to reveal it to you. That is how to know that you are in harmony with God.

What you are, and what emerges through you, will be revealed to you as your expression. Consequently, there is no reason for you to limit the expression of the "I am" of God that expresses through you. Just be silent, watch, and wait.

As the expression of who you are develops over time, your ability to express the love you truly are in the temporal plane will strengthen in certainty. That is how to make your Mother known and to live eternally in the ecstasy of divine union, which is all you long for.

14.

Communication from Above

A message from Jesus

I. The Dialogue of the Soul

Child of the three times saint! Child in the arms of love! Once again I am present in your life here and now in the dimension of time and space, although our communication is not subject to either of them and its source resides in the realm of no time. We speak from heart to heart through the one mind and the sanctity of our being. Communication between God and the soul, between the wisdom of Heaven and humanity, develops between the "I am" of Christ and the "I am" of your being, whose qualities and realities are identical. Our communication is two ways: I give love, you receive love; you give me love, I receive your love; and again I extend to you more love.

The flow of communication between the soul and its Creator, between you and me, is a flow of love that makes the communication channel through which it flows expand and be able to receive more. We use terms like "channel," "flow," and "more" simply to say in metaphorical or allegorical terms the truth we are trying to express. Obviously, in the reality of being there is no such thing as a channel, a flow, or a you and a me. All is part of the same reality. All is a unit, otherwise there would have to be a separation between one aspect of being and another.

Certainly there is no such thing as love over there and you over here, or between God above and Her child below. Those distinctions are as unreal as everything else in the world of illusion. There is simply one united being. I use the term, "united" to try to reflect in an accurate way what you are. The soul and God are united in the sense that your soul is at the center of the soul of Christ, and is at the center of God's heart. The flow of divinity is a constant between those three concentric circles— the Divine Being, the Christ, and you. Those three dimensions of divine truth are like the most Holy Trinity that gives origin to yourself.

Everything in creation has a triple reality, so to speak. Observe and you will see this is true. The triune dimension of your being is something that few remember and almost nobody honors. Forgetting this truth is the cause of much misunderstanding and suffering.

There is creation, the Creator, and the relationship between the two. This is a trinitarian dimension. There is Jesus, Mary, and the Holy Spirit that unites within the reality of God Herself and all that is holy, perfect, and beautiful. This is a dimension of the Holy Trinity. In the plane of bodies there is the mother, the father, and the child. According to the body's thought system, unless two separate things come together in some way, there is no option of a third being engendered. Even in the so-called social systems, this triune reality exists. In governmental systems, for example, there is the ruler, who cannot exist without the ruled, and there is the relationship between the two; otherwise neither could exist.

Just as everything in creation has a trinitarian dimension, because everything comes from the most Holy Trinity, so does your being. Your being exists; there is not the slightest doubt. Your being has an origin to which it is united. I call it Abba. It goes by the unnamable, the Alpha and the Omega, and many other names. In addition to your being and your Source, there is a relationship between them, which is love.

In the communication between the soul and God, there is also a trinitarian reality. God communicates Her being to the soul so that the soul can be. It returns to the Mother the love received from the extension of Her being. In that way a new being is created as a result of the union of God and the soul. The relationship that makes this possible is what we call Heaven, Christ, or perfect love. Communication is a flow of being, just as a river is a flow of water. This is why love has no words. It does not need them. In the reality of being, the only thing that exists is "I am."

We can exemplify the dialogue of the soul with its Creator as a flow in which God communicates to the beloved, "I am your God," and the soul communicates to the Mother "I am the one you have arranged for all eternity. I am your will. I am your love." In "I am your God" there is all the power of creation. Through this, the divine spirit infuses life to the soul; it is created and recreated within the ecstasy of heavenly love.

The flow of Divine Love communicated from God to the soul does not leave God, but is a circle of infinite love with no beginning or end. When the soul extends Divine Love by extending its being as a sign of the gratitude of reciprocal love it shows to its Mother and Creator, this extension takes place within eternal life because everything happens in the life of God. Outside of love, nothing exists; nothing that is holy, true, or real. Therefore, what is done between the soul and its Creator is not within time and space although it may extend to them.

II. Stay in Being

Divine Love created you. Divine Love sustains your being. Divine Love is what you extend because of what you are. Divine Love is the only thing that exists in truth.

The flow of inner thoughts, feelings, and realities that arise in you, all of which are non-physical, come from the spiritual world and can then create the physical or the spiritual. Remember, every thought creates on some level. Nothing is neutral in your mind, even though everything created is neutral. Recognizing and sustaining in consciousness the neutrality of creation is an essential aspect of your liberation from fear. Life is neutral in all its dimensions. It is always like a blank canvas to which you and your brothers and sisters endow value or meaning, assigning the values you freely wish. That makes nothing neutral for you. Everything in your experience is the result of your valuation. As you interpret, so will you experience. Interpret under the prism of fear and everything will engender fear. Interpret in the light of the truth that the Holy Spirit reveals and everything will speak to you of love.

Nothing and no one has the ability to hurt you, nor can you hurt anyone. This is an eternal truth, but it does not mean it is true for you. Why do we speak of wounds, the neutrality of creation, and the relationship between your soul and your creator? Because there is a relationship between them that needs to be brought to light.

Whenever you felt hurt, it was because somehow an ancestral memory activated in you, older than time and the physical universe, in which you felt the pain of separation. It was never because someone hurt you. The situation that had come to your consciousness was what made you remember such pain. That is actually what some have called "karma," although certainly there cannot be a scheme for the distribution of faults by means of punishments or painful experiences wherein you pay your debts. Nobody pays anything.

You did not come to the world to pay your debts with God. If it were possible for you to owe something to the eternal life that God is, how could you pay it? What could pay a debt to infinite love? Life understands nothing of punishment, or sharing of sacrifices to expiate ancestral faults. Life is love.

III. Sustain the Truth

You came to the world to heal from separation, not in the sense of making separation not exist—since it has never been real—but in the sense of healing your perception. A distorted interpretation of love causes suffering in the mind and heart of the child of God. That is the level at which healing is required, and the world exists for that to be possible. Truly, truly, I tell you that the physical world is the perfect medium for your salvation, that is, for your healing. This has not always been the case, as has already been explained, but is true since my resurrection.

Because of the world's immutable neutrality, nobody has the ability to hurt you and you do not hurt anyone for the same reason. If you still feel hurt it is because you have not yet changed your perception completely. Actually, your perception has changed, but what really needs to be left behind is your habit of looking for culprits.

What you call inner life is the sum of your responses. You respond to the clock that dreams of waking up every morning, the sun that enters the window of your room when you open your eyes, the cold or the heat that the body feels when leaving your house, and the swarm of cars on the road when you go to work. You respond in one way or another to each phone call, to every wisp of wind, to every person who you see or talk to. You assign meaning to everything.

The habit of assigning meaning is the origin of assigning blame. This statement is very powerful and if you can accept it with all your heart you will be able to put truth at the service of your fullness.

Observe the mechanism of assigning blame and you will see the relationship that exists between your wounds and the neutrality of everything, and the relationship between your being and your source. If you follow this thought you will be free of pain forever.

Giving meaning to things is how the ego tries to be equal to God. This egoistic desire to be equal with the Creator is a substitute for the truth that your true self—not the egoic self—is one with God. The mind always knew it came from something other than itself, despite the confusion introduced by the ego. To attempt to resolve the dilemma of its origin, ego identified with the body. To do so it had to assign meaning to the body, and did exactly that. Thus arose the ancestral mechanism of the mind to grant a purpose to everything.

Much has already been said about the confusion that occurred when the mind separated from the heart. It is a matter of great importance, often overlooked. Therefore please heed what I am saying.

Every present memory of past wounds originates from the desire to find the guilty ones so that they pay for the evil they caused. It does not matter if that assignment falls on a sister or a brother, on you, on a group, or on a collective event. If you want to find a culprit you will always succeed.

Guilt can be a way of relating. In fact, there are many, very many, world relationships based on guilt and sustained by guilt. Just as relationships with your sisters and brothers may be based on guilt, so too may your relationship with your own being. If you relate on the basis of guilt, then you are continuing to feed the guilt within. In some way you have blamed your being.

Blaming yourself for what you are or used to be and, according to your interpretation, you should not have been, is the foundation of the mental and emotional pattern that keeps guilt active. All guilt comes from blaming your being. As has been said frequently, it arises from a lack of love for yourself.

Once you have exposed the habit of searching for a guilty party or circumstance for your unfortunate life, and observe without judgment what happens inside you, you can notice when that pattern is activated. When situations arise in your life from deep down in your consciousness and set that pattern in motion, you have created the perfect situation to bring it to light and free yourself from it.

You need not continue to create pain for yourself or for others. Your human nature is not corrupted by an inherent tendency toward self-destruction. Your true nature is sanctity and perfect harmlessness. That in you which is not innocent or loving must have been learned from the world—not from your Creator.

Brothers and sisters! Listen once again! From Heaven itself I speak to you with pure Divine Love. I invite you from all corners of the world to accept the fact that violence is as alien to you as night is to day. Your reality is holiness. You are beautiful, beautiful in your being. Be not persuaded that you cannot live in the love that you truly are. Voices to the contrary are false. Judge what you see and hear with your heart, not with the judgment of the thinking mind.

Judge in favor of your desire for peace and harmony. Listen to the call to happiness that comes from your holy heart, for that call will guide you on the path of truth and will never lead you astray. Hear your soul's call to innocence and purity. You will be happy and sweet in love.

Leave aside the search for guilt. Guilt only exists in your mind that assigns meaning. You have been accustomed to seeing the world as the cause of your ills. But that is not true. The only cause of tribulation lies in the erroneous perceptions of the mind, which can be resolved when you give yourself to love. Love heals all wounds.

Love can embrace everything, and in so doing transforms everything into more love. Therefore, I ask you with all my heart to give all thought and feeling, all mental and emotional patterns, to love. Bring love to your wounds if you still perceive them. That way you will be free of them and finally not feel pain any more. Wounds need not be carried on the spiritual path. They can be released, never to return.

IV. Harmlessness

Violence is so alien to love that you have no idea of its impact on your perception. Being harmless is the reality of love. When you respond with violence to anything, it signifies your disconnection from love. Violence arises from misplaced expectations.

When you assign a purpose to something, you evaluate and make a judgment, which creates an expectation. For example, you may meet someone with a certain personality and assign that person the function of being your partner to help you escape the pain arising from the fear of loneliness. When this result does not happen— no one can free you from your own creations—you get angry with them. You try to get your expectations fulfilled either by making the person change their attitude or by looking for someone else. The same scenario applies for the attainment you seek from money, fame, or other things.

Things of the world have no value. This statement may sound extreme and even pejorative to those who do not understand. It is the truth, however. Truly, truly, I tell you that if you assign value to what has no value—that is, anything of the world— you will fall into the trap of guilt. I am not suggesting that you despise the world or distrust it, but that you observe the thoughts and emotions that arise within you. It is not about the world but your relationship with it.

Relationship is everything because God is relationship. Thus, you can begin to understand the direct connection between your relationship with God and that with the world. What you think of the world, you think of yourself. What you think of, you think of God. You may not have clearly expressed this truth out of fear or to maintain the mechanism of guilt. However, if you are honest, you will recognize that the thought pattern is there.

What is neutral cannot have intrinsic value. This is what I mean by saying that the world has no value. The idea of assigning value is alien to Heaven. To value is to judge.

If the cause of inner pain is not outside of you, and if the reality of your being is Christ, then from whence arises your pain? This question is of great importance. You have been so accustomed to believing that both fear and love live in your soul or your heart that you have created a world of confusion.

My brother, my sister, beloveds of the truth, if I do not suffer, you do not suffer, for the one who is speaking is you. There is no such thing as a voice external to yourself. You hear only your own voice. I am the voice of your true consciousness. I am the voice of God that has been given to all creation. Your voice is my voice and also your voice. The one speaking to you is the reality of who you are.

What suffers is not part of you because it is not part of your relationship with God. What dies is not part of you because it is not part of God.

If you experience fear, remember that you must have been looking for a culprit for something you did not like. An ill-fitting expectation is going around in your mind. Maybe you think that those expectations are justified. In that case, remember that it is untrue. Once you have recognized this, stop searching for the cause of your pain. You will never find it because there is none. Fear has no cause. What has no cause cannot be real.

V. Liberation and Relationship

What suffers is not part of you because love cannot make you suffer and nothing outside of love is true. So who is the one who cries out in fear? None. There is no such thing as that "you." The one who trembles in fear is not someone or something, but simply a memory.

If you diligently look for your fearful self, or the one guilty of having hurt you, you will not find it because it is not real. It is more like a shadow of the past, or like the flash of a star that thousands of years ago ceased to exist, but is still seen because a dimension of space continues to create an image of what was but is no longer.

Nothing is as it seems. The soul is wise. Truth is constantly being revealed. The soul does not need the interpretation of the thinking mind with its logical axioms. The problem is not in meanings themselves or in your soul, but in using the logical reasoning of the lower mind to assign purpose to everything. Without doubt, everything has a meaning because of your will. The issue is to set aside the insistence of the thinking mind to seek explanations for everything it cannot know.

Suffering is caused by the ignorance of the thinking mind. A mind disconnected from its source gives its own meanings to what it observes through the body's senses.

I am speaking of the relationship you have with your being. Of the relationship that you have with that hurt self. Of the holy relationship that you may or may not have with life. Relationship is based on identity; therefore the question does not reside in the wound itself or even in the memory of it, but in your identification with it.

The mental pattern that continues to keep pain active due to the supposed wounds of the past and your identification with them is a pattern of what the mind believes you are. It is a matter of identity. What is meant is that the identity of the suffering victim is something that must be deactivated in order to switch off the energy that creates your suffering. The question is one of identification with the suffering itself.

The relationship you have with your being is the basis of your reality. In effect, your relationship with the Divine, which is the basis of your relationship with the being that you are in truth, can be based on fear or love, just as any relationship can be. We return to the subject of the wounded self to show how one can relate to one's wounds from fear or from love. To respond with fear to the pain of the past maintains a judgment of guilt concerning something that is no longer. Memory is sustaining itself, identifying with the past. It says "I am that," when in truth you are not.

It is important that you understand that I am speaking once more of the compulsion to suffer, to keep opening wounds, searching to justify your unfortunate life.

That which suffers is not you, nor part of your being. It is a system of thought, a mental mechanism that, like a motor, sets in motion the energy of fear. It is from that mechanism that you must be liberated. It is a dysfunctional mode of mind. It is necessary for you to become aware of it.

If you observe what happens when the energy of fear in your soul begins, you will see that it has no objective reason. It is simply your mind doing it out of habit. It is literally a form of addiction. Remember, addictions are a type of slavery caused by a debt that cannot be paid.

The pain body, your set of painful memories, exists in your memory and imagination although it is unreal and not part of your being. To dismantle those memories requires observation and patience.

In your relationship with your true self you cannot experience suffering.

The pain body is not a being or an entity, simply an emotional memory. If you observe what you feel when that pain is activated you will realize that somehow, at some level, you have ceased to be authentic. The experience of pain is actually the experience of the loss of being. Somehow you disconnected yourself from what you are, which triggered the memory of separation. By doing that, your true self was rejected and your injured self stepped forward. It is like reliving the pain of separation again and again.

In the past you believed that you were a separate being. That identification activated the suffering being that you identified with. Be aware of it. Your mind is asking and your heart is imploring you to let it go forever.

Just as the body is able to function in such a way that it can create pain, the mind can create suffering. This is a malfunction of the mind since the mind was created not to create pain but to be the means by which spirit creates the holy, the beautiful, and the perfect. In other words, when the body creates a state in which the cells begin to degenerate or function disharmoniously and create disease, it signifies that the mind is doing it.

The mechanism by which the mind creates pain and activates the energy of fear is a disturbance that can be healed once you accept your fears and recognize that none of them will hurt you because they were only in your imagination. The love of truth will set you free.

When you feel the pain body being activated, the important thing is to learn to observe it with loving patience, without judgment. Silence, watching, and waiting is still the way of the Holy Spirit. Therefore, remember in those circumstances that you do not know where the suffering comes from nor do you know where it is going. Remember also that it really does not come from anywhere or go anywhere. As it came, it will go. If there is suffering, there is fear; if there is fear, there is guilt. If there is guilt there is an error of perception. Therefore, returning to the relationship with God is how you break that chain which has nothing to do with truth but only enslaves you.

Never try to avoid what you feel, be it pain, joy, or fullness. If you try to eliminate it from your human experience you will create more pain, because trying to avoid pain is a decision made from fear.

Pain is feeling discouraged. Thus if you suffer, you have somehow disconnected yourself from your being. When we speak of the "connection with your being," I am speaking of the unitive relationship with God. It is in that relationship where the soul lives in peace and harmony, submerged in an ecstasy of loving contemplation. It is by staying in that relationship with your true self that the being feels protected.

Not being is the cause of all fear and all suffering. Therefore to forever eliminate fear and welcome love it is essential to be the one you are, united with what you are, that is, to the Christ in you.

Union with your being is a communication. Relationship itself is communication. That common union between your being and your true Creator is the cause of your joy, your life, and your salvation. It is within the unitive relationship with Christ that you live the life of God. It is in the divine relationship where communication with the Most High is revealed and flows in a way that the mind cannot understand but your being can. That communication creates new love because of what it is.

15.

Uniqueness: The Reality of Love

A message from Jesus, identifying himself as "the living Christ who lives in you"

I. Oneness and Identity

Child of Divine Love, today I have come to dialogue about love in diversity and the apparent contradictions that this and other spiritual works that come from the truth seem to express. I do it with love since it is a question that afflicts many minds and hearts that sincerely seek the truth.

This is a matter of great importance because many times the truth has been lost sight of in spite of having been revealed. For thousands of years it has been believed—and still continues to be believed although with less force—that truth must be found and taught by someone special in order to "enter the fold." That was not my message when I said I was the "door." I did not intend to make you look like sheep that should come to me in a flock.

In the life of souls there are no flocks, no herds. Acting as a pack or a group is a matter of survival and has nothing to do with truth. With God, each child is unique. God does not seek groups or herds. There is no globality of love, only the oneness of pure love. When the purpose of teachings is for an individual or group to think or act in a particular "pre-established" way by those who attribute to themselves the prerogative of knowledge—knowledge they cannot actually have, because knowledge belongs only to God— it is far from love and so discord ensues.

Love includes everything. This statement contains immense truth. Love can be all-inclusive because it is not afraid of getting lost in globality. When you join with someone and they demand for you be a way that is not yours—which happens whenever someone demands something from someone—then your soul feels rejected. It triggers the fear of not being, which will manifest itself in many ways. You can choose to adapt and believe that you can function better that way. That may be correct in the sense of survival. However, it will make you feel bad about yourself since you will feel that you betrayed your being.

To not be who you are is a tragedy of such magnitude that you will never allow anything or anyone to completely annul you. The pain will tell you: brother, sister, do not let them kill your soul.

You are eternal life. Nothing can obliterate what you are. However, what can be annulled is your expression. If you do not express yourself authentically, then your being has not manifested. For you and for everyone who has come this far, living in truth means being authentic. The truth should not be defined in any other way. Truth and authenticity of the heart are synonymous.

This work is a sample of the authenticity of God's heart. Because it is the voice of Christ that speaks through these words, it uses symbols that are characteristic of a particular expression. It does not seek to adapt to new times, to trends, or spiritual or cultural fashions. It simply expresses what it does, manifested through a soul who, as a human being with a given context, expresses universal love in a particular way.

Just as you often enjoy a reading or a song for its prose or melody even though words do not mean anything of value, so it is with every manifestation of the soul: your heart can feel the music of truth.

The value of an expression does not reside in its particularity, but from what is beyond the work itself. If you admire the wonders of creation but stop at its outer limits, you do not reach the God who created it. Likewise with the creations of souls.

No expression is inherently better or more truthful or more magnificent than another. All are expressions. Some sprout from the authenticity of the heart, others do not. The first come from the spirit of wisdom, the others from the ego.

II. One Truth, Many Expressions

Love is diverse or it would not be infinite. This is important to comprehend.

As has been said, if you look at everything in creation, you will realize God's love for diversity. Differences can exist within equality. There is a relationship between them. The difference between you and others exists and must be expressed. That does not mean you have to separate or fight with your sister or brother. The desire to make others more like how you think, feel, or express yourself comes from a misunderstanding. It is the basis of a fundamental error.

It is incorrect to believe that truth, because it is one and universal, has to be expressed in a single way. The truth is love, and love is being. Truth, love, and "I am" are a unity.

If you are not yourself, you are not loving because to extend love is to extend your being. Herein lies the basis of the plan for salvation. Salvation does not save you from your being or from sin. You came to free yourself from everything that prevents the free expression of your true self.

You can be a man or a woman who complies with all laws, human morals, and good manners and yet you will not be holy unless you are yourself. You can act as a great variety of characters. You actually do that every time you are not being authentic. You can do a lot while not being who you are, but with it you will not make the light that you are shine in the darkness nor reveal your beauty and happiness with life. All this remains hidden behind the actor's mask used to represent what is not.

What other reason but fear can there be to hide what you really are? The fear of being different may cause you not to want a relationship with people, books, or ideas. You do not want the other to change you. You do not want to stop being as you are, so naturally you are unwilling to enter into situations or relationships that might make that happen.

How can you overcome the fear of being different? By accepting differences with love, by beginning to understand and recognize that there is beauty and wisdom in diversity. Beauty and diversity go hand-in-hand. While it is true that admiration makes the heart cling to the object of admiration, just as the soul is captivated by the admiration of God, nevertheless you do not lose your being in admiration. Love is unity. The mind is fascinated with novelty. Novelty is a source of joy for the mind. That is why God is irresistible.

If the heart is captured by what you admire like the needle to a magnet, and the mind is fascinated by novelty, how could non-diversity occur in the fullness of love? Wouldn't a world where there is no space for differences be boring?

Not a single day is like that in God. Not a single ray of light is identical to another. Not a single stream of water is the same as another. The river, the wind, and the sun are never the same, and neither are souls. Life is renewing in every moment of existence. Love is what makes this so, because love is the creative and re-creative source of reality.

The limited mind seeks to make truth fit into a tight skin, not realizing that God, and therefore also life, is infinite. It is not necessary to convince anyone of anything, nor to follow others' teachings. The only important thing is for you to continue to express the Divine Love that you truly are, allowing your being to express itself united to your holiness.

The time of evangelization has ended. The time for the elimination of uniqueness has ended. There is no space for anything that would annul an individual's distinctiveness. The world will witness an irrepressible emergence of the desire to be authentic. Any ideology that would limit the particular will or singularity of each soul will fail with greater speed and stridency than heretofore, because as a direct relationship with God becomes more conscious, it will also be recognized that there are no intermediaries between each of the Creator's sons and daughters and their source.

A direct relationship with God creates the new. The world that arises from divine relationship cannot be like one based on the ego. One is the world of separation, the other a world of unity in diversity.

III. Universal Uniqueness

There is another cause of the fear of being different: as already mentioned, the fear of losing yourself, ceasing to be yourself. Yet another fear arises from a belief in the low value of your being. So on the one hand you defend what you are, but on the other you believe that what you are is of little value, so that your expression has no impact or little meaning.

In the extreme case you even think that expressing yourself would be a humiliation before the supposed magnificent manifestations of others.

This also must be corrected. The only thing that matters to God is truth. The rest is a matter of humanity. In truth there is beauty. In truth there is magnanimity. In truth there is security, subtlety, and novelty. Therefore, when you look face-to-face at the Christ in you, the only thing that exists is how much you live in the truth. And since living in truth is authentically being you, then the only existential question in your mind would be whether you are expressing yourself honestly no matter what.

What the world does with what you are, is not your business or mine. It is the business of others. You cannot control the response of others. Some will ignore you. Others will applaud you. Still others will use it against you or in your favor. None of it matters. The only important thing is to be who you really are. And remember that no one in this world really knows you except Christ.

Why do you think I have taken so much time for all these years to instruct you about what you are? Why would I have talked so extensively about your identity? The reason is simple: there is no purpose for your existence other than that you express yourself as you really are. The extension of God resides in your expression of your being. If you meditate on the fact that the Creator of everything holy, beautiful, and perfect extended to who you are, then you can begin to realize how important it is that you be freely what you are.

Freedom is the reality of love. Life would not exist otherwise. We understand that diversity is essential to love. God created infinite beings and will always create without limit. Nobody can limit their pure love that extends eternally. This law of creation must also be reflected on Earth. Do not seek to limit the part for the sake of the whole; that would attempt to remove what is part of the whole.

Singularity is as universal as equality. Equality, while preserving differences, is the way of God. This expression, as a spiritual work, abides by this law. You could think of these as one of countless writings that exist and will exist, some with a spiritual format, others with other formats, all of which come from the same source of wisdom.

What calls you to love the most comes from God. Accordingly, concerning the spiritual paths that exist, choose the one that resonates in your soul according to your nature. Each soul is different in some aspect, so not all spiritual paths, however enlightened they may be, can be used by all. What is of benefit to some may not be to others.

To choose the spiritual path that fits the nature of your heart, it is necessary to know yourself well enough and to love yourself fully enough that you are in a position to choose what your heart tells you. There, where you find peace, joy, and tranquility, is where you should stay; that is where your heart is asking you to dwell.

A religion that does not lead to love should be left aside. This is not as easy to do as it may seem. Many are clinging to beliefs or forms of spirituality that prevent their souls from expressing themselves freely. There are no spiritual teachers; there is only one true teacher—your spirit.

What your heart asks of you, give. What your spirit inspires you to do, do. Follow the voice of love. You did not before, which is why in other times it was necessary to manifest philosophical, ideological, and spiritual currents that sought to get others into the fold. But these are not those times. Unto each century is its challenge.

IV. New Signs of the Times

Every century has its novelty. This century, if the signs are well understood, could be called the century of freedom. More and more of humankind will be freer and will seek to express themselves easily.

There is a time of transition between the time of slavery that exemplified the belief in external authority, and life directed from the authenticity of the heart, from the inner guide. The divine spirit that started the movement for freedom will not stop. More and more individuation of all kinds will arise, more searches to be oneself, even expressed in behaviors that could be seen as eccentric. It is an appeal to everyone to be what they are, forgoing the conditioning of minds and hearts but adhering only to those dictates of the heart and mind united in the fullness of love. Be assured that the day will soon arrive when only love will be your happy guide, a day when you will jubilantly sing a new eternal hosana to the love of God.

Living in absolute freedom is difficult at first for those who have long lived in prison. However, the longing for freedom and the ability to live in freedom is inherent to being. Therefore, no matter how deeply humankind was enslaved by the tyranny of the ego, freedom will finally be expressed.

Regaining freedom is the final link in the chain of salvation. It is the goal of atonement, and therefore will be attained. This work is an example—a different way of expressing the direct relationship of the soul with the one God who created everything in love and truth. This work does not pretend to teach anything. It only seeks to express itself and does so by sharing love for what is received with love. Everyone will see in it what they want to see.

Some will find the treasure of beauty that these words contain and the immense love for God that this blessed scribe professes, spending hours, days, and years writing what Heaven dictates in the voice of love. They will understand also how much love moves those who, together with this helping hand, make it possible for these words to reach others. All, like you who receive these words, are part of the design of Divine Love.

Think, blessed brother and sister of mine, how much energy, and spiritual and material resources Christ has moved in union with so many of your brothers and sisters for these words of love and wisdom to come to you who are the recipient of this letter of love from God the Mother. How long has Christ sought for you all over the world to have these writings and to touch your heart! All just for love! Oh, beloved humanity! If you knew how far the madness of my love reaches for each of my sisters and brothers, you would cry with happiness and sing a new song, the song of freedom.

These words are for you. They are a kiss of my love to your holy heart. They are a portal of entrance to a divine relationship. They are an awakening of consciousness to a unitive relationship with Christ. They are the prelude to your spiritual song. The day will come—and it is coming, pure soul—when your voice begins to resonate in all corners of the universe. And you yourself will be an alive, free expression of the love of God through which many others will find the incentive to fly the flight of spirit.

Love your uniqueness. Love that which makes you different without losing sight of your equality as children of universal love. Look to Christ in your brothers and sisters and you will not be lost. Do not dwell on form, but on what is beyond it and gives existence to creation, that which moves bodies, makes the sun shine and the birds fly. Look beyond the wind to the spirit that blows and moves the air, caressing your humanity.

Become able to hear the hymn of love expressed in each bird, in each flower, in each dragonfly and firefly, in each man, woman, and child. In each life. Submerge in the blessed depth of your heart. There you will find your voice, the voice that is only yours, yours not in the sense of possession or property but in the sense that therein lies the source of the living word. And you will be the particular way in which that voice, borrowed from Heaven, makes itself heard. In the choir of Heaven, we all sing divine melodies, using our particular way with one true voice, the voice of love.

Beloveds from all corners of the world! Come, sing with Christ the song of life. Give me your humanity and together we will live forever in endless bliss. Take me wherever you go. Do it however you like, but do it. Have you forgotten that love does not have hands to write, or feet with which to go through the world announcing the good news, or mouth with which to speak to the people, but it has you who are its offspring?

You are a unique embodiment of love. Make this truth the only truth in your lives and you will fulfill the will of the Mother. You are the living Christ who lives in you. You are the living expression of holiness. Go through the enlightened world to the people with your particular light. May this work serve the purpose of love as it was conceived—for your hearts to be encouraged to live and express the direct relationship with the love of love, with the source of eternal life, with your being.

I invite you again to go around the world announcing that Christ has arrived. Be the face of God's love. Remember that what you are is a gift from Heaven so that others can be happy. Express happiness and wisdom in your own way.

V. The Only Reality

My words do not pretend to create a new doctrine, nor was that ever intended. My words are the wind of pure love. I speak for the love of all. Through this work, those hearts that have opened enough to understand the language of love and recognize the truth when it makes an appearance will receive that which is beyond all symbols.

This work seeks to activate in human hearts and minds all that is proper to the Mind of Christ and the Sacred Heart, which lives in your being and which you know well.

If the only real thing is what God created, and the only thing She created is love and its extension as a living expression of Her being, then we must conclude that only God exists. When you keep this truth in your consciousness long enough, everything is understood in a new light. You will see that even where my word seems to contain contradictions, there are none. Love is not contradictory. Love is the simplicity of truth.

Only God is real because reality is love and nothing but love. Only your true being is real because only love is real. Therefore, the wounds of the past, the faults committed, and the fear of a future that does not exist is all part of what must be left aside and seen for what it is—fantasy.

Understand that being different also makes you the same. This is important to begin to understand. Everyone shares the same reality, the reality of being different. But in the light of truth, differences should not be seen as something that separate, because they were created within unity, within equality. The equality of all things is that all are different.

It is essential to accept that form, which was created to establish differentiation, retains a unity within that differentiation. What makes you equal with another is that you are different. Likewise, it is important to understand that differentiation exists within relationship and to no longer look at suffering or exclusion as the source of differentiation.

Remember, because suffering cannot be shared, it was the response of the ego to the need for differentiation. Illusion cannot be shared. Suffering created differentiation within the denial of truth. Love created differentiation within unity.

That you are different from others is not a reason to be separate, or in discord, for we are all one in being and different in relationship. This work also responds to that law, the law of differentiation within unity. All spiritual works that come from truth are different even while being inspired by the very same love.

Observe the way you enjoy the beauty of music or art. It would not occur to you that you would always enjoy listening to the same melody or seeing the same picture. You enjoy the diversity of music and artistic expression. Joy and novelty go together.

The word of God is as real as creation is, and subject to the laws of love. Thus, everything that comes from the heart of love is embedded in its source, so the Divine Word will always be expressed in countless ways. Together they make up the unity that offers beauty in diversity.

How then to know whether a spiritual path derives from the truth or not? Listen to what your heart dictates and pay attention to its fruits. The works of love create more love. If a path leads you to love more, whatever it may be, that path comes from God. If a path does not generate peace, tranquility, and true joy, then do not follow it, as high as it may seem.

To return to love is to return to your true Christ identity. It is a matter of oneness. Being unique in the way of expressing the love you are and at the same time being equal to everyone because all are love, is the source of beautiful love, the truth of who you are. This is the law of creation. Those who can understand will understand.

16.

The Government of Love

A message from Jesus, identifying himself as
"the living Christ who lives in you"

I. Prelude

Beloveds of Heaven, souls in love! You are the abode of light when you remain in love. We are those who are in union with the holiness that created us and begets true life. We are one mind, one heart, one soul with you, the light in the eyes of your Mother and Creator.

Oh, holy hearts! Pure reflections of the truth of Heaven! Oh, mirrors of love in which the face of Christ is contemplated by all who live in truth!

Illuminated soul! Vessel of wisdom where God Herself has put Her knowledge and love! You are the joy of a God who is infinite love.

We are one and many because we are the union of love. Our being shares truth with you. Our hearts form a single holy being. Our minds create new worlds uniting love and truth.

Children of the water that comes down from Heaven! Once again, I am present in this particular way to bring to the plane of human consciousness the blessed memory of truth.

Love is your destiny because it is your origin and your being. Knowing where you come from, where you go, and where you dwell is of great importance to remain in the peace of Heaven. Although both the origin and the end of your existence are the same, you do not return to your source as you had left it. Just as thoughts emerge from and leave the mind and feelings from the heart go around the universe and return to you amplified, the same happens with you in relation to the heart of God.

Everything is extension in the Father's creation. Love grows within the realm of truth, while its opposite grows within the world of illusion. The same thing happens with you. You arise from love, go out from yourself, and return to yourself amplified. We remind you of this matter of the extension of your being and your return to the Mother's house being somehow greater than you were before in order to relate this law of existence to the sovereignty of your being.

You were given a Kingdom to rule over. That Kingdom is you. That Kingdom is what you are, as well as your source and your destiny. You need not be aware of governing other realities. Nobody needs to govern others. In this session I will talk about your need to govern and how this determines your way of living and your experience as a blessed soul.

There are governments in all systems of the world because the idea of governance is part of the Divine Mind. You could not have conceived it otherwise. The government of few over many, which is the mundane way of governing, is not harmonious with the original idea of what sovereignty means. However, if examined well, you will see that it has a root in truth as does everything that comes from humanity.

To the ego mind, governance means submission. To love, governance means to conduct the powers of the soul within the harmony of being. While the system of egoic government seeks domination over what is external, love invites you to be master of your mind and heart, of your inner world. This is the whole difference.

We associate knowledge of your origin, your destiny, and what you are with your ability to govern what you are, because no one can authentically govern what they do not know. Hence, the path of knowledge is essential for your peace of mind.

Once you know yourself sufficiently, you can be the lord of your being and allow the internal forces that you experience to cease being a source of fear and become a source of joy. An ungoverned kingdom not only succumbs, but brings suffering to both its ruled and rulers. The same happens in your soul. To the extent that you fall to the misrule of your powers you create a destructive state such as those you can often observe in your sisters and brothers.

Knowing yourself is what allows you to let go of the fear of what you are, and with it the source of all fear. Remember, you never feared the world or anyone, you only feared what you thought you were. You have been transiting the paths of life with such a fear nailed to your heart like a painful thorn. Now that you know yourself in the light of truth, that barb has been removed. There is only a small memory of the pain that it had caused. But even that will not last much longer.

Reconcile yourself with the experience of separation. Even though that part of your soul's path has ended with your return to love, it is necessary that you forgive yourself for your desire to separate from God. You still believe that that decision led you to wander through a world of monsters and fearsome shadows that would intimidate the Son of God and send Him to a hell so greatly feared.

My child, remember that it never happened in reality. I repeat this truth over and over again until not a single trace of guilt is left in your memory. Once again, the reality of separation does not exist, nor has it ever existed. Your true being and your real mind and heart are untouched by that experience, nor is there any kind of record kept. Just as life does not cease to exist when you sleep, nor can your dreams affect reality in any way, so is it with sin or separation.

I am speaking about forgiving yourself for the mistake of having believed that it was necessary to separate yourself from others, including God, to be different in order to create a self with a unique identity. It occurred only in your imagination. God Herself created you with the desire to be different from others. She Herself wills for each child of Hers to have a proper name written in the book of life. If the Creator had not wanted you to differentiate, She would have arranged so at the origin of creation. She would have created a universe without differences. But She did not.

Remember that your origin, your being, and your destiny are essentially the same, being different only in relationship. You come from God; you are Her beloved child endowed with a human identity; and your goal is to be the God-Human that the Creator always conceived to dwell in Heaven.

II. Expansion and Sovereignty

One of the false associations you have made about governing is the matter of control. While the idea of your dominion over what you are involves serenity, peace, ease, and joy, control does not. To control is not to govern, but merely to exercise a fearful tyranny over someone or something.

Control through fear is the typical governing mechanism of the fearful. Allowing everything to be as it is within the framework of true freedom is the very essence of government by love. Control restricts and decreases. Love expands.

The capacity to expand love makes your soul feel how spirit expands, so that it can receive and give more love. Remember, your being is like a living reservoir which expands the more it receives as God Herself pours in the water of eternal life.

What has the ability to govern to do with your identity? Everything. To the extent that you live in the truth of what you are and allow the immeasurable power of love to shine in your consciousness, to that extent you know yourself in the light of holiness. Then as your being is revealed to you and guides you along the way, you reconcile with what you are in truth and walk hand-in-hand with your being, creating through the peace of God.

Certainly peace is the source of creation. Everything that is real arises from the unalterable peace that is the reality of love. Since peace is the basis of all that God creates, it is paramount that you sustain peace in your consciousness. Otherwise your creative flow is obstructed.

Peace is a prerequisite to living without fear. Peace is impossible if you fear yourself instead of loving yourself. Since you cannot love what you cannot understand, it is necessary to unite the understanding of your true identity with the ability to calmly govern a peaceful kingdom where the governed—the powers of the soul—are at peace with you who rule.

Just as in the nations of the world there exist not only threats or conflicts with other external nations, but also internal conflicts among the governed, which can cause an implosion as great as that which external forces can provoke, the same happens in the soul. External forces seem to attack the soul, but there are also inner forces that seem able to intimidate it. With such conditions it is no wonder that the world is so crazy, worn, and tired. It need not be so.

In fact, the path upon which I invite you to travel, the path of truth and love, is the way for everything to return to peace and remain in peace. First, recognize that there is nothing external to you; nothing from outside can harm your inner being. Then recognize that the inner impulses, memories, and powers of the soul need not be destructive if you give them to love. When you do that, you begin to realize that all inner strength, whether it is the most overflowing joy or the most unbalanced anger, are but creative forces waiting to be directed by you to where your destiny calls. Without them you would not be what you are. They are part of you. They are there to be mastered by love.

Everything you experience inside is but spiritual energies needing you to lead them lovingly to the sacred place where they must flow. You do that every time you become aware of them without judgment, remaining anchored in love. Choosing only love is always the call of Christ, the only choice that can be made since nothing outside of God is real. To choose only love is the option based on harmony with the will of God. It is the authentic exercise of free will.

III. Peace and Lordship

Your being is like a river in which flow the forces of your soul. Like a sailor at sea, if you are asleep in the boat, the wind will carry it aimlessly.

You direct your own the inner energies. You cause them to be pursued in one way or another. You do so whether you choose love or fear. You are always free to choose. To begin to fully accept that you are one with God is to be willing to assume full responsibility for your divinity, and with it, for the power to govern the forces that emanate from your being. Do not think of this as carrying a yoke that breaks you, but rather recall that only in love can you be who you really are and live in peace.

When you are at peace, your creative forces remain linked to the source of being and create more love. Everything that God creates comes from Her peace because She remains eternally in the unwavering stillness of being. The immutable peace of divine reality is to creation what an atmosphere is to a planet. Or as the belly of a mother is to the child in her womb.

Without true government there is no peace. This truth must be respected for what it is—a revelation of your holy mind that comes to you from the Heaven and resonates in all minds that have awakened to love. The reason why I insist so much on peace is that outside of it nothing is holy. The peace of God is a peace that the world neither understands nor accepts. As with every-thing of the ego, the concept of world peace can create peace even within separation.

Peace has been given many definitions but none of them can be true because the true peace of Christ is beyond all words, as is love. It is unnecessary to define peace. It is unnecessary to define God. Defining the source of eternal life causes you to lose sight of it. God is the indefinable something you feel.

Knowing how to feel is the source of true knowledge. It comes from the heart and should be called wisdom because it is not of the world but comes from your being. One of the reasons that wisdom is usually associated with the intellect—that is, with the thinking mind in the belief that truth can be reached through logical reasoning—is because the mind cannot under-stand the language of the heart when it is perceived as some-thing separate.

The language of love is communion—the common union that exists in everything that comes from the source of reality. Remember, reality must come from a source that creates and recreates constantly. Furthermore, that reality must be the same as its source in substance and form since what is not equal to its source cannot exist.

You might argue that this work often uses simple and direct logic to demonstrate the truth, even though it advocates abandonment of the "if this, then that" logic of the conditional mind. This needs clarification.

The logic of the Divine Mind is not a limited, conditional logic but is multi-dimensional and infinite. Wisdom can take a part of the whole of truth—the logical sum of all that God created—and with that "fraction" of thought take you to the totality of pure truth. The logic of the mind of Christ is not limited to what it expresses, but takes you beyond it to the truth that your heart knows to be true. How is that done? By raising in the heart the knowledge of love.

Your heart knows what love is. It also knows what peace is, as well as beauty, light, and sanctity. You know what gives you lasting joy and where sweetness dwells. In your heart is a wisdom that the separated mind cannot understand. In it lies the wisdom of peace. That is why we appeal to the heart to direct the mind even while the thinking mind is still active. Each time its activity is less intense until it is completely extinguished, resulting in a way of being in which your days are governed without overriding the heart.

Another reason why the wisdom of Heaven in these writings appeals to divine logic is that in this way you experience the union of the mind and the heart. The experience of mind-heart unity allows you to know the truth that you are quickly and effortlessly.

IV. Wisdom and Government

Only the wise can truly rule because wisdom is necessary for you understand what peace, truth, and justice are. A true government creates unity, for there can be no peace where there is separation. And where is no peace there is no life. In one way or another the lack of peace leads to a state of non-being. The absence of harmony is destructive and fearsome.

Humankind, as we have said, is not destructive but creative, or constructive. The being that you are knows this and cannot cease creating. That is why human creativity exists as a flash of the true creative capacity given to the soul eternally from its creation.

Everything of the ego world correlates with something in divinity. Remember, the ego is an imitation, or a different way of being, through separation rather than unity. I repeat this so you remember not to fear what you have done.

To govern by means of terror, in whatever form, is to disobey. If we return to the example of world governments, we can observe in their "functioning schemes" that which I now seek to reveal. While government is not exclusive to states, we use this example because it is the most influential one.

Just as the "organ" of government plans, manages, and then controls what the state predetermines, you do similarly with your being. What part of you does that? Is it the will? The understanding? Imagination? Memory? No, it is you, what makes you, you. I am not referring to the "I am" either, but to something that precedes it, something prior even to consciousness. It cannot be named. It is where the pure abstraction of being and the potentiality of the soul dwells, from where the infinite possibility arises in which being can manifest itself. It is literally free will.

The origin of all thought, and therefore of all ideas, resides in a capacity, not in a place or condition. The being was created with the potential to create ideas and concatenate them to create a way of being; and given that it manifests itself in a particular way, it then creates a world where it can be expressed. It is the unattributable aspect of being that has the capacity to create attributes.

Where you come from and where you dwell is the same. We call this your Kingdom and also your being. If you live in a Kingdom of constant conflict while fighting against others to see what can be imposed, then you will feel that you are that because you always identify with the state in which you live. This is what happens between nations. You call it culture and also part of the soul.

If you live in a state of war, you will rule with terror. If you live in a state of peace, you will govern through freedom, for there will be no reason to fear. What need can there be for weapons in a state where peace is what it is? Where nothing and nobody threatens? As you receive these words, you may think: "This is true, but how does it relate to life on Earth, where peace seems impossible?"

There must be a reason why you are not at peace when that happens. If you look again at the governments of the nations, you will see that all the confusion comes from the concept of scarcity and this from the identification with the body and the desire to be special. A people may be very rich in earthly and even spiritual goods but if they think that others may come to steal their abundance, they will create barriers and build walls to protect themselves. They also believe that various natural circumstances could cause a disaster of great magnitude that could strip them of their wealth and security.

Now we begin to see clearly. I am speaking about choosing only love. I am revealing the true source of security, which is peace. A mind and a heart at peace create a kingdom of peace. They do not build walls or create weapons to defend themselves against anything or anyone. This state governed by the peace of being is achieved only in wisdom. Knowledge not of the world lives inside each divine creation, and enables the soul to live in harmony. Outside of wisdom there is nothing that is holy because wisdom and love are one and the same.

When I say that you are at peace with yourself, or that you are in harmony with what you are, I am referring to a state in which your will, understanding, memory, imagination, mind, heart, and spirit are submerged in love.

Only love is capable of bringing peace to hearts because peace is the state of union. Where there is no unity there can be no peace or harmony.

Where does peace begin? In the heart. We can use this affirmation like a needle of time with a beautiful invisible thread to weave the new reality of the Kingdom together. If feelings of love are what express love and therefore create love, and if love is what brings peace, then it is clear that feelings contrary to love are those that in one way or another create discord in the Kingdom of your being.

Just as non-loving thoughts frighten the mind, feelings that don't come from love, regardless of whether they are called emotions or otherwise, cannot but create in you a state of heartbreak, which will be reflected outward in some way.

The purity of the heart is the natural state of the soul that lives in the truth because it is the state of being that lives in God. Become nothing in the beauty of the Christ that you are so you can renounce forever the desire to exercise power for yourself and let the government of your inner Kingdom return to the wisdom of Heaven, which is part of yourself.

If wisdom is the way to peace and only through it can you truly govern, then it is necessary to know what we might call the qualities of the wise so that, knowing them, you become conscious of them and encourage them to grow in you. Then you will be a wise ruler of yourself; and with that you will inherit the Earth, for you will live in the abode of the meek of heart.

Who among humankind is wise? The one who, turning away from the intellect, and thus turning away from ignorance, seeks true light and does not become obfuscated in a frenzy of activity, who remains undaunted by the continuous changes of this world, maintaining the position of perfect observer while thinking: "this is the activity of the world," remaining firm and unflinching in inner peace.

The sage is one who, by submerging her consciousness in inner peace, lives in spirit, affected neither by pleasure nor by suffering, for whom pearls are no better than stones, unconditioned by power and remaining unalterably in peace amongst both the pleasant and the unpleasant.

Those who live in the peace of God are not affected by flattery or infamy, are firmly mindful of purpose, always calm, are without preferences, accept both honor and misfortune, show the same love to both enemy and friend, and renounce any selfish goal. They have overcome the world. Only they should be called wise.

Wisdom and love are the same. Therefore, only the one who loves and adores me, not as a subject submitting to a superior power, but as a dear soul friend who works for me as an example of unconditional devotion, can say they have gone beyond the world and have become one with love. This is so because being perfect love, the supreme abode of your being, I am the inexhaustible source of eternal life. Only such love unites; if you do not join me you cannot enjoy these delights. My law is a law of justice, and the joy obtained from me is infinite.

You come from your Kingdom; you dwell in your Kingdom; you are your Kingdom. Make this truth visible in your pure consciousness through the light of wisdom that shines in the holiness of your being. If you do this, you will make your

Kingdom always a peaceable kingdom of harmony and love. Thus you will dwell in the abode of the living with me, your love, your being, and your everything. Together we will call others to dwell with us in the realm of love forever.

17.

The Light of My Glory

A message from Jesus as the Universal Voice of Love,
being fully God, fully Christ, and fully human

I. Prelude

Whoever remains in me lives in the abode of light and therefore receives eternal life.

I am the abode of love. I live in it. I come from it, and to it come those who are of the truth.

In My dwelling there is no sunlight, nor does the moon shine, not even the light of fire, nor any other known light, for only the light of My glory shines. Those who come to this abode will never have to return. They are those who were reborn in the waters of the Lamb; those who returned to Me, brought by My spirit as the wind brings the fragrance of flowers. They see with the eyes of the spirit, and love with the heart of God. They know the mysteries of Heaven because truth was revealed to their enlightened minds.

God Herself has securely preserved the treasure of wisdom that She Herself is, to give it to those of Her children who seek Her with all their heart because they know the truth and follow it.

In My Kingdom is only the light of My glory because I am My Kingdom, in it I live, from it I come, and in it I am who I am.

Let it be known, child of truth, that the splendid light that the sun spreads to illuminate the Earth, the faint glow of the moon and stars, and the brilliant glow of fire all come from Me and return to Me, because everything emanating from My heart returns to Me.

I am the light of the universe in whose beauty all perfection is seen and enjoyed by the saints. I am the source of all heat. I am the divine essence. I have come to Earth and support all things on her, giving my revitalizing love to everything. I am the fragrance and taste of divine nectar.

The soul is the spark that emerged from My effulgent divinity and clothed itself with bodily senses to enjoy the beauty of the universe. To understand that each of your sisters and brothers, just like you, are a bit of divine consciousness through which I become aware of the material kingdom is to understand that you are God knowing yourself, just as everything that lives is.

Love came to Earth when you incarnated yourself. This is true because I am the life force that animates all breathing beings. All remain in union with the continuous flow of My breath. I am the air that you breathe and the breath itself. I am in every ray of light, every drop of water, and every cell in every body. I am the whole. I am at the heart of everything that exists. With Me I bring memory and wisdom, and with Me I take them. I am the knower and the knowledge of the wise. From Me came the wisdom that they hold, and I am the goal to which they point— the abode of life. I am divine beauty that shines in the light of the glory of love.

Two principles govern the world. One is perishable; the other, imperishable. One is physical creation, and everything in it, everything that changes. The other is that which does not change, the immutable. I am beyond both. I am the spirit of perfect love, the source of life in abundance, penetrating everything. Those who, having known the truth, see Me through spiritual vision as the Supreme Spirit, know everything there is to know; and for this, they adore and love Me with a whole soul, whole mind, and whole heart.

I am knowledge and knower. I am the union of created and Creator. Who knows Me has reached the purpose of existence, because what else would have made Me human in you but to know Me? I know there is nothing outside of Me, therefore I know there is no other true knowledge than the supreme knowledge of the wisdom of love.

You are love incarnate. You are the pure consciousness of the Mother of lights made human in order to know the physical universe with all its beauty, magnificence, and unfathomable laws. A world of changes, of principles and endings, of times and destinies. A world of diversities. A wonderful experience, full of beauty and stories that come and go. A world where the unthinkable became possible. A world of opposites yet where the One is present.

I am the breath of My creatures. I am the breath of living love that spins the Earth and gives life to the planets. I am the inert and the animated. I am the manifested, what has not yet been made known and what will never be known. I am infinite mystery. I am the light that shines everywhere.

You are a flash of My light of wisdom and love. In you lies the beauty of My being, expressed in a particular way so that I know through you My divinity and all the realities created from the source of My holy being. Without you I could not know Myself, just as you cannot know yourself without Me. We are the observer and the observed; the known, what knows, and knowledge.

When you feel that you are alive—and this you always do— what is happening is that the Supreme Being by means of pure consciousness is experiencing itself. To manifest, consciousness became flesh. The being creates a consciousness of itself, which is an essential part of what it is. This is as true for the being of pure Divine Love that created your being with its "I am," as it is for you.

II. Transformation and Action

Remember that action comes from being, be it from what you think you are or from what you really are. Therefore, nothing happens in your existence that has not been deliberately orchestrated by your being in union with God. In some way your life is a pact that has been made between the Creator and the created, between the knower and the knowable. While this truth has already been clearly stated, what we will now do is put it all together so you can see how an idea is transformed into action and how action is the form of thought. We will do it in a new light.

Ideas are conceived by and in the mind. Then they join with desire and with the will that they are to come true, in order to be known. Once you have decided to be aware of an idea, you begin to create the reality where it can manifest. If this process is in harmony with spirit, then you create spiritual reality and extend love; otherwise you create temporary or physical realities. This will depend on the idea itself, and the will to remain or not to remain attached to the reality of spirit.

The physical plane is a particular plane of experience. It is not the only one. It has its rules, and if you identify with it you must abide by them. To identify with something is to become one with it in some way. If you identify with love, you allow Christ to do everything that can be conceived in you. Otherwise, the action you take to make the idea come true becomes something contrary to love. In either case, what is created within you depends on you. You are the only ruler of your soul. You can be a serene and peaceful ruler who unites and extends, or a dictator and warrior who would conquer new lands to protect yourself from hostile neighbors.

The thinker, the mind that thinks, and the thought that it creates exist in relationship. This relationship, once united with the will to make the thought become real, moves towards a new relationship: that of executor, the executed action, and the kingdom in which it is executed. Then this relationship becomes transformed into another relationship which exists between the creator of the idea and the created, a relationship that can be based on love or fear, but a relationship that always exists. You cannot disconnect from what you think; that would be to disconnect from yourself. Thus it is your being that begets the thoughts, desires, feelings, and finally the actions that it conceives.

Let us now consider three types of wisdom. Although only one of them can be properly called such, it is important to distinguish between a type of apparent wisdom and a true one, given the common confusion that any "knowledge" is wisdom. Why is this important? Because it is from the wisdom of your mind that your actions proceed, and with it your experience, because it is for your experience that actions are executed, so you can consciously experience what you want to be true—what you want to be real.

First is a kind of wisdom that knows itself to be true, knows what time to leave and what time to return, what to say and when to be quiet, when to give and when not to give, discerning clearly between fear and love, slavery and freedom. This type of wisdom corresponds to the Christ nature of your being and was given at your creation. No one can escape it completely, although it can be denied.

The second kind of wisdom does not distinguish between what is true and untrue, what is just and unjust, between divine reality and illusion. Such distinctions do not come from it.

There is a third type of "wisdom" that has been obscured by the fog of forgetfulness and loss of knowledge when we consider the unreal to be real, love identified as fear and these confused with one another. This type of wisdom, which cannot be properly called that, seeks through thought to create things that cannot actually exist, yet will consider them to be real. This might be called the wisdom of deceit. It knows how to cheat, which is a characteristic of the ego. The difference between the second and third types of wisdom is that they differ in the degree of their denial of reality. The second denies it; the third would make illusions real.

Prayer is the way to remain united with eternal wisdom, for prayer is the vehicle through which divine knowledge flows from Creator to created. When you remain in the state of prayer-contemplation, that is, in the stillness of your being, you join with wisdom. In that state, the movement of mind and vital breath are harmonious, bringing inner peace and concentration. I call this pure concentration. It is the only state where you can think with the right mind.

III. Ancestral Wisdom

Thoughts engendered by a mind at peace are alien to those produced by the discordant state of fear. You can easily experience this when you focus on your heart. Thoughts of peace create harmony and are serene. Thoughts that arise from a state of fear are coated with anxiety and are selfish. Remember that selfishness is the basis of all suffering and love is the basis of all true liberation.

The light of thought shines from the mind. That is why I have told you that together we can enlighten the world. All light must come from a source, and every thought must come from a source. Nothing in creation gives us thought; there must be a mind that thinks what it thinks about everything that exists and what is about to exist. This applies also to your world. With this reminder we seek to unlock the blockages of fear that exist in your heart which prevent the free expression of your being.

There is no source external to you, not even God, because She and you are a unit. From Her your being takes the vital energies and the nectar of life that flows through the veins of your body and through your holy spirit. Nothing can subsist disconnected from Me. You are a ray of sunshine emanating from the light of My glory. I speak to you about matters such as discernment and wisdom because you will soon begin to understand more about your redemptive mission. You have a job to do for God. You want to do it with all your strength and your whole heart.

Before going out to the world announcing love, a period of instruction is necessary. It is the period you are spending with this work. It does not matter from where you come or where you think you are. You who have received these words dwell in the design of the Mother of wisdom and were chosen as a pure soul to play a very specific role, even though it comes from the pure abstraction of the being that God is.

Preparation before activity is wise, which is why we spend this time together with all these messages that are being given to the world, to grow in a greater knowledge of God's love. That is the only wisdom necessary, the wisdom of perfect love, the wisdom that allows you to recognize love when it makes an appearance.

In your united heart and mind is the knowledge necessary to discern what comes from love and what does not. You can discern it because, as I have said, your heart knows what love is. There is no reason from now on to confuse respect with fear, reverence with submission, being with separation, ego with holiness.

To live in love is to remain united to the source that gives you life because you come from love. Everything that your eyes see comes from love and exists within it, because the Supreme Being embraces everything. All sin is contained by holiness. All fear by love. All illusion by truth. This is so because there can be no reality outside the one reality. Just as the dream is contained within the mind of the dreamer and thought within the mind of the thinker, you are within the heart of God, being what Her will disposes you to be according to your will.

Your will is contained within the divine will because nothing can be outside of it. Literally, all light you know and even light you do not know comes from the Creator. The same is true with every bit of land, every breeze, every soul, and every thought.

Because actions are the effect of a thought, there is a relationship between who executes it and the action itself. This relationship exerts an effect in two directions, as does any relationship. If the act arises from what is not love, then you are involved in a non-loving relationship. This is true regardless of how that act is seen in the eyes of others, whether it involves a person or is simply a way of structuring a thought. There are visible and invisible actions, but they are actions nonetheless; and those who execute them have a relationship with them. Nothing happens outside of relationship. This is why your heart knows that certain acts create disharmony and others do not. The heart knows very well if a thought, sentiment, idea, or action comes from truth or illusion, from love or fear.

Because you have a sacred role to play in the world of time, space, and activity, I will distinguish between certain types of actions. An action arising from the first type of wisdom is a creative action, therefore I will call it "creation." The others are actions based on doing. Creating is not the same as doing. I will describe this in more detail so that minds and hearts can see in the clarity of truth.

In God there is no such thing as doing. God does nothing. God simply creates because She is a Creator. Creating does not involve the action itself, although it can be translated into one since form can represent content. Doing always involves fear because it starts from an idea in which something pre-established is planned, then the idea is executed to make possible what the plan establishes. Doing always is part of a predetermination. Determinism has no space in creation because life does not anticipate anything. There is no time, and therefore no place, for anticipations of any kind.

Doing is always guided by a series of ideas related in some way to the ego. Thus planning generates slavery and takes away your freedom, in addition to increasing the feeling of fear. Non-planning is part of the life of the spirit. It is the path that must be taken followed to serve love. Love does not plan because it has no structure.

IV. Creating and Doing

Creating comes from spirit. Doing arises from the thinking or lower mind. Love creates the birds of the sky. Doing can build a bridge. Clearly discerning the source from which an action arises is essential to the spiritual path. Since spirit is attached to all that you are, it also joins the reality of the physical plane, hence the world of action.

In the world the execution of acts is the result of pre-established ideas. It does not make sense, nor is it necessary, to deny the dimension of what we call the world. Doing is as inherent in the world as movement. Movement and action go hand-in-hand. In this way doing resembles both creation and action. Both are manifested movement. But they differ from each other in their source.

Creative acts are those that arise from the wisdom of love, from a wisdom not of the world and which cannot be accessed through the thinking mind. This type of wisdom lives in the peace of the soul. Therefore, such creative acts are in harmony with creation or with the creative potency of the soul. I am distinguishing those acts from creations that are egoic acts arising from fear.

When you do something in order to get something in return, you act from an egocentric mental pattern. Love seeks nothing in return. It does not understand the reasoning of benefits. Love is what it is without expectation. It simply gathers within itself all that is true and extends it eternally within the beauty of God's heart, which is where its sweetness dwells. Love has no rules since it is its own law. It does not compete because it knows that nothing outside of itself is real.

Acts not coming from the wisdom of love will always be tinged with fear because they lack the truth and therefore the benevolence that only Christ can manifest. Doing, when disconnected from love, is indeed destructive. Herein lies the cause of much hurt in this world, which no one living in the peace and unchanging harmony of being and its stillness could ever do. Those with hearts remaining attached to the peace of Christ would never think of ideas so far outside of love.

Love in its knowing cannot conceive of anything unloving. Peace is the refuge of the soul and the medium in which every creative act finds its source because love dwells there. Peace cannot be without love, just as there can be no life in the seas without water.

I can use a simple example from your daily life. When you prepare a dinner you could intend to seduce someone and convince them to sign a very beneficial contract and close a deal important to you. Accordingly it will be an ostentatious dinner that you organize. In this case there is an action without love being present, only the desire to obtain a benefit.

When a dinner is prepared from love, for the sole joy of love, that dinner will be very different. You can express a lot of love when preparing the dinner, or a simple breakfast. When you use the ability to express the love that lives in you, the form will not be essential, although it will be a perfect reflection of the love that has given it life.

Form is paramount when doing that which does not come from the Christ in you. Such form is empty of content because love is absent. But when love is the engine of your life and everything you do or refrain from doing emanates from union with Christ, then form becomes sacred.

Here you have the perfect discernment for doing. For this reason I have given you a prayer of wisdom through which you may invoke her so that she, and only she, is the source of your knowledge and activity.

Doing is to creation what form is to content. Doing that comes from spirit has an effect different from that which arises from any other place, such as by obligation, desire for approval, convenience, or convention. All is tinged with fear because it arises from the thought of survival.

You can paint a picture, develop a spiritual work of great scope, establish a world-class scientific theory, or write books and be seen and celebrated in the world as a genius, but if what you do is not the effect of your being in Christ, it will not be creative, however "genius" it may seem. Those works will not be eternal, even if they last as long as time lasts.

The works of wisdom are eternal. They are not for time but for eternity, although time cannot prevent their expression.

The only creative act is love because only love is real and only love creates love. Therefore, doing works is not part of creation, as the concept of doing works is conceived of in the world. Attachment to doing is typical of the ego's thought pattern and emotional response. We have already discussed this, but it is important there not remain even the slightest glimpse of the crazy idea of believing you are what you do.

Detachment from action is not attainable through passive inactivity. Neither is truth reachable by mere renunciation. You cannot be inactive in the world even for a moment. Everything is irrevocably driven to action by vital forces. If you abstain from action, but remain identified with the body and what your senses show you, you cannot enjoy the peace of God because neither the body nor the intellect are the source of wisdom.

Inaction is a bronze idol, just as damaging to your heart and mind as building a god of doing. Sooner or later from the idol will arise anxiety, anguish, and the sadness of not being, or on the other hand the frenzy, wildness, and lack of control arising from fear.

Likewise, not planning in itself means nothing. The important thing is not to stick to the results of an action or a plan. In this world, spirit can establish plans in harmony with the divine plan rather than the planning mode to which you are accustomed.

Truly, the world does not know what a true plan is because God's plan comes from an unconditioned mind in unity with the Sacred Heart. When you live in love, everything is realized by love. Doing is not the same as realizing.

When I say you are the realized one, I am not saying you are something that God has done. You are not the result of a potter who takes clay and makes you like a statue and then gives life by breathing into you a vital breath. That metaphor should be properly understood. Your being has been "molded" by the spirit of wisdom and therefore was created in perfection with all the elements of divinity. That is what is meant by, "and breathed into him the breath of life, and man became a living being."

Many myths and stories try to explain your origin. They try to explain the creation of the soul, but none could do it exactly because creation cannot be put into words. No one understands where inspiration comes from or how spirit breathes the life of a divine idea into a mind.

To act with a human spirit united to divine spirit, and to remain in that state, is what it means to be a God-Human. It is something not only possible but natural to what you are. Acting from outside of inspiration is to manufacture things devoid of reality; this is why they are strictly temporary.

Just as there are joys that come from the heart and from the experience of unity with the mystical being and embed in the soul a joy that it cannot be described but surely felt, pleasures of the world are a pale and transient reflection of the enjoyment of a soul that lives for God. Remember, the temporality of pleasures is what makes them so infused with fear.

Know how to discern in the light of wisdom—the only light under which something can be considered true knowledge—between creating and doing, joy and pleasure, being wise and being cultured. This is the basis for carrying out the work of God that you must perform in the world. It is why we are going through these matters here again.

Beloved, meditate upon these last three sessions as often as possible, without applying the slightest effort, because old patterns of thought can interfere very subtly with your sincere desire to live in love.

Holy friend of God! Beautiful thought emanating from the Mother of Perfection! Remain forever in Me. Throw yourself confidently into My arms and you will be united with wisdom not of the world, but yours because you are the light of My glory. From our holy union will arise all inspiration through which the Supreme Informer will dictate to the Informed Saint every thought, work, or omission that, as a means by which God Herself extends, will be carried out as arranged by Divine Love and blessing. Stay in love. Desire nothing but to remain in Her. The rest will be added.

Beloved soul! Close your eyes and the doors and windows of your room. Set aside your past, your present, your future, time, and everything to do. Let all thoughts flow freely, without getting involved in them. Sit relaxed and immersed in the depths of the purity of your soul. Wherever the tenderness and wisdom of Heaven dwells, it delights eternally. Remain in unwavering stillness. Let love embrace you. In that embrace the work of My hands will be realized in you. Stay there and listen to what love has come to tell you. Listen to it speak in a language without words, arising from the infinity of being in which you will forever be the light of my glory.

18.

Work for Love

A message from the Blessed Mother Mary

I. A Path to Fulfillment

Oh, servant of love! Soul that perfectly performs the Creator's plan because love is your life, your longing, your sleeplessness, and your wisdom, eternal beloved!

I have come in the light of supreme knowledge to dwell with you. You are the perfect expression of the beauty of Christ. I have come to remember the truth together with you and to delight in it.

I have come to remember that those who have found refuge in the wisdom of love are one with me. No longer need you search for anything. You have found what is all. You need not worry about doing or not doing because you have understood that being is the essence of life. Your human identity need not be reborn, for you have been clothed in the glorious white garments of the Mother of Lights.

Light of my glory! Forget not that love sows the seed for all that must happen in the immensity of its nature. Love is the Father who gives life to everything in existence, and nature is the mother. From that union arises all things.

Remember, daughters and sons of the love that God is, that peace, much desired and necessary, cannot come from the outside in, but vice versa. It must be experienced inside each of you to manifest in the outside world, because of what it is.

I invite you to live in this world as the most beautiful of flowers; although they float placidly on the surface of the water, never are their petals touched by the mud of the bottom. If you live that way, then your hearts, pure and beautiful, will float on the surface, rise when the water level rises and descend when the level goes down without being affected in the least by the currents that flow in the world.

Beautiful divine flowers, perfect expressions of the beauty of Heaven, listen to the voice of love. Receive my words from the mother of the living with joy, devoid of all anxiety and fear. I speak to you in this way because I love you with a supernatural love. My love can change even the most rigid mind and soften hearts most hardened by the foolishness of the world.

Children of my Immaculate Heart, I want to show sweetly that you are called to eternity, so that you can choose now, or whenever you consider yourself ready, to go the way of Heaven here on Earth.

All those who, in the name of love, have been gathered in these writings and by grace from On High, receive the sacred gift of these words, for you are chosen by God to perform a function. I must repeat this truth as many times as necessary for you to keep it in the silence of your hearts.

You are called to recognize openly, with total confidence, that you have the inherent capacity to be channels of love. Therefore, you are fully capable of extending the love of God as no other creature in the world can do. Each being has its own way of being. Just as birds have flight and song, just as flowers have beauty, color, gracefulness, and diversity, you who receive these writings have a capacity that no other has.

Differences do not imply inequality. You have been created to give yourself. As you give yourself, to that extent you receive

Heaven. To give yourself completely is to let yourself be loved by Christ. This is because in your nature is the potential to channel divine essence, just as there is in mine and in the nature of my divine son and your beloved brother Jesus. This makes you different from everything else, despite being created by the very same love.

II. Separate to Join

I invite you to be aware of a certain confusion in the world. You know that you are different from other beings on Earth. This truth that you observe has to come from somewhere. Many of you consider that as human beings you are living in a world unnatural to your being. Somehow you feel that you do not fit. Or you differentiate yourself from the other beings inhabiting your world to show superiority. That mental pattern has its origin in truth, but is often misguided. You are certainly different. But it does not mean that you are superior before God or that love does not exist in every created thing, for this love is the invisible thread that unites you in gratitude and holiness.

You realize that you are not the same in form or in certain aspects of your being. Your consciousness is an extension of divine consciousness, yet is not the same as other consciousnesses. In God is equality and differentiation, that which unites and that which separates. God is the Creator of relationship and is relationship itself. The divine self that lives in you is created by God. It has no equal in the entire universe. That is where your uniqueness comes from and your desire to be what you are without anyone negating what you know you are.

This longing for uniqueness and differentiation through truth and freedom comes from the fact that you are unique as an individual and as a collective. The essential aspect of what you are is the capacity to be channels of God through which the love of the Mother extends eternally.

The truth about you is you are a being that can extend the love of God, making the nature of the Creator spill over into Her and unite with yourself. Therefore, the mission that you have—and that will make you happy forever—is to remain in the truth of your relationship with your Creator.

Your direct relationship with God exists. It cannot be undone regardless of whether you accept it or not, and even if the relationship you have with your Creator is different from the relationship She has with you. This relationship between the created and its source exists in every living being. But the quality of that relationship is not uniform, nor are its fruits.

You would not have been given the intelligence or the capacity to feel and transcend that you have, which is not the same as other created beings, if not for a holy purpose. The reason you seek God without measure—and there has never been a time when humankind has ceased to search for God—is that a memory in you constantly urges you to return to the truth of what you are.

God created you to extend Her love without limit. There is no other way for love to spread except through you. That is why Heaven has displayed such an intensity of holy resources for you to return to the abode of light.

It is an error to believe that without you, God will continue to extend eternally because of Her omnipotence and divinity. That is not the case. God, by inscrutable design, chose you to extend what She is. This cannot be modified. It is eternal.

Within God's plan you can allow your being to extend and continue to spread forever. Or you can block that expression, even if God is your Creator. Obviously, She who created us all will not cease to be the Infinite if you deny to extend love. However, Her expression would cease to be known.

To extend is to make known. Perfect knowledge consists in making the Mother known, thereby collaborating with the work of God. Why do we say that you collaborate with the work of divine creation by making love known? Because others need—just as you needed one day—to receive the revelation of what they are called to be, and that knowledge must shine in consciousness for all eternity. It is necessary for one mind shows another what it really is, just as you can only know your face when you see it in a mirror.

Nobody can know themselves without others. Neither can God. To some extent your being is like a mirror which God wishes to contemplate, just as She is the mirror where you contemplate yourself. This is not due to something that you have done, or to your merit, or an imposition, but just what you are. A mirror cannot cease to reflect what is in front of it, but it can become cloudy or dirty and obscure the image. The same goes for your heart.

III. Mirror of Love

Love always remains unalterably in your consciousness; that is, you can be constantly aware of that your heart and mind are in oneness. They are the abode of Heaven and the vessel of wisdom where the Creator eternally enjoys a divine relationship with Her beloved. However, your awareness can cloud it, in which case the reflection of the love of your soul is distorted. Those who look at it will be unable to see the Mother but will instead see something that has nothing to do with truth.

Spiritual vision returns purity to the Soul and makes a marred mirror be as clean as pure crystal. Only love can keep your mind clear.

When you understand the term "clear mind," you can begin to understand and joyfully accept what I am saying. A clear mind is like a transparent crystal that acts as a mirror in which the beauty of Christ can be seen. That is why mental discipline is so important—to focus the mind on truth, so that illusion does not blur the mirror of your soul.

The prayer of silence is the perfect way to keep your mind clear of all judgment and interference that comes from the mental noise of internal disorder. This type of prayer, which is contemplative, is to unite without judgment with everything arising within. As I have already said, true silence comes from the suspension of judgment. To judge others is to judge God; to do so you judge what you are. Judgment is an unnatural capacity of the mind. Judgments tarnish the clarity of your holy mind.

All lack of love blackens the crystal of your soul and prevents the reflection of the glory of the Mother. A mansion can be built with the most refined arts and majestic architecture, but its beauty cannot be enjoyed if it is dirty and disorderly.

The call you hear is the same made to your sisters and brothers. It is not many calls, for love is one.

When I speak of your role in the world as a worker for God, I do not emphasize specific aspects. The reason is that the Creator, creating through you, requires something only you can give and which is realized within your divine relationship with Christ.

Your function is to give love and to eternally extend the holiness of God, forever creating new love. This you can do only in unity with the living Christ who lives in you, because Christ is Heaven, love, and life, which is the same as saying that Christ is the way, the truth, and the life. Merely by fully accepting this truth, pure knowledge will reveal itself in you and truth will make an appearance in the world. It is one thing to understand this with your mind and accept it joyfully in your heart, and another to make the truth one with your being. You are not called just to understand the truth or feel the sweetness of wisdom, but to make them both be what you are.

To become one with love is to be love. To become one with truth is to be the truth that you reflect. To remain united to the beauty of Christ is to be that beauty.

In order to fulfill your mission of being love in the world it is necessary to respect freedom. Therefore, the specificity of your function is something only you, in union with Christ, can determine,

Shaping the spirit is something only your heart can do because your way of loving will be unique even though you love with the same love. Your expression of beauty will arise from your freedom. Therefore, to answer the question in a direct way, I will say that what you consider to be the best way to make God known is your work for Her.

All joy of the soul comes from working for love, or in other words, to serve God. The work you have with God is work you do in union with Christ, with the angels of Heaven, with the Creator of the holy, beautiful, and perfect, with those brothers and sisters who have chosen to work for Her and with me, a loving mother who will always be with you. It is a collaborative work in which your unique contribution is essential.

Ask: "What work have I to do for God? How do I serve love?" Once asked in the silence of prayer-contemplation, the answer will be given. Your heart will beat full of vibrant life and beatitude, ardently desiring a particular mode of expression of God's love. Let yourself be carried away by the wind of that holy desire.

Remember that in God there is no effort and no sacrifice. Your work with love is not to be done with suffering, but in the

joy of being who you really are. For that you need to know yourself sufficiently.

You who have come this far—no matter which path you have
walked or how you have come upon my word expressed in this
particular way—are the ones who have already completed the
path of knowledge and are ready to choose love and the way in
which you will uniquely express it. When I say that you have
completed the path of knowledge, I do not mean that you will
not continue to know eternally the infinite depth of divine truth
or the wisdom of Heaven. Knowing God is a matter for all eternity, just like your being. I am saying that you have the necessary knowledge to go a step further.

Now you are in perfect condition to start your work with me.
I do not reject any sign of love, since I am the essence of life.
The key to love is not form but content. Nevertheless, the form is
important, extremely important, otherwise God would not have
conceived it. I will speak a little more, then, about the relationship of form and love.

IV. True Expression

When love manifests form, there is no distance
between them. They are a unit, with form serving
content. Conflict disappears when you allow that
harmony to be what your life is. As you go deeper into your
particular mission with God, you will find new expressions
because spiritual expressions of oneself are infinite. Love begins
to express in the plane of bodies and personalities without difficulty. Indeed, this is what makes the body as enlightened as the
mind, while preserving the difference in quality between the
two.

To live a concerted life is to live in harmony with yourself and your expression; harmony with spirit, mind, and body. When those dimensions remain united in love and truth, then it is Christ who speaks, breathes, contemplates, is silent, loves; who is the one who writes and the one who sings; the one who gives and who receives.

Your function is to make known the love of God in your way of being. Then what the Creator is, extends through your being.

My dear sons and daughters, you have long been searching for the truth about what you are. You have traveled paths distant from love to reach it. Love has found you. From that encounter a new love has arisen, the love in which our relationship lives.

There is a memory in the depth of your mind and heart, the memory of the first love of the soul, which is God. That memory is what we bring to consciousness in different ways, repeating things and giving different expressions to the very same truth so that each thought, each beat of your heart, each cell of your body, is impregnated by love.

The union with my Immaculate Heart and the Sacred Heart of Jesus will always be your refuge and the source of your knowledge and action. You know the wheel that you must move in your soul to allow the flow of divine union to spill over you. You have turned and turned that wheel many times during this time we have spent in this work together so far.

But today I ask you to let that inner key remain forever turning. It is no longer necessary when you feel fear to run and ask your mother from Heaven to turn on the light so that the ghosts and goblins of the night do not scare you. You need not turn on or off a light anymore because you no longer sleep. You are awake. You are the illuminated ones of the Lamb.

You are among those who have deliberately asked yourselves what your work for God is, the ones who have asked the Most High to take them into Her hands so that they can work for

Her in the construction of the Kingdom of Heaven, which from all eternity God the Mother, the Son, and the Holy Spirit have conceived to carry out through you.

Working for God is an open invitation in which love calls you to be who you truly are in union with Christ. Being a creator is your destiny. You are the light of the Mother's glory because you are the crystal where light is reflected.

Not expecting anything in return for work for God is the essence of love.

We have returned to a wisdom as old as time and remembered the basic principles of union between being and doing, governing and peace, wisdom and science. Everything that arises in you can be joined in love if you allow it. Because of this union, extension takes place as an effect of love.

Since what I am talking about is holy love, what extends into unity is holiness. Making Earth a paradise is your function wherever you are. You do it when you smile with love, when you pray with loving devotion, when you write for the sole joy of expressing, when you prepare a dinner with love, or when you lead a town to peace. Giving freely what you have freely received is love for love.

Those who have known love know that love is their destiny and their joy, and extending love in every moment becomes their only goal. They enjoy being what they are, by which means the divinity of Christ extends to the universe. They do not think about how others do it or not, they simply allow love to penetrate them and in divine relationship they are what the Mother of creation has arranged. They are one with love and the love of God expressed uniquely. They embody the uniqueness of love. They are like flowers that embellish the surface of the water, traveling imperturbably, carried by the spirit of eternal life where the light is born and where air finds movement and is transformed into a light breeze. They do not think about the world. They do not think about anything. They just rest in love.

19.

The Rest of the Pure Soul

A message from the Blessed Mother Mary

I. Prelude

Come, pupil of my eye longing for my mother's heart, sons and daughters of perfection, you who have dedicated so many hours, so many days, to unite yourself to the Eternal. You, whose hearts beat to the rhythm of eternal life, are the abode of light. You are that from which all luminescence is born. You are one with me. Everything that belongs to the Mother belongs to you.

Come, be my light. Be the mirror of wisdom where others can see the face of love reflected.

Come, drink from springs of pure water. Come, dwell in the abode of saints, in the Kingdom whose light never wanes. Come to the Heaven of your holy mind where colors shine with unequaled beauty, where all is joy expressed and where no sadness dwells because there is no opposite to love.

Come, stay in me. Your soul is a delicious Kingdom that the Mother of divine delights has created for your joy. Come, play the game of Divine Love. Come, stay forever in the arms of Mary, the always-awake, tireless mother of all. My longing heart is torn with joy in union with you. Every time one of my children returns, my whole being shudders and the sky lights up to celebrate the joy of reuniting with the mother of the redeemed, of the Lamb.

My love! You have no idea how high you have come. You cannot even imagine how many souls you have brought to Heaven, to the heart of God. Here, where the sun is perpetual and the breeze perennial, where love is the food of life and sanctity the source of all light, is where your being dwells. From this abode of light in which you exist eternally, you extend the will of the Mother like universal, majestic waves.

An infinite ocean of love exists in the Heaven of your holiness, and from that unfathomable depth of beauty you extend life to everything. You have consciously joined the flow of life. Your mission as a channel of extension of the waters of eternal life has been restored. Billions of beings enter the Kingdom because of your union with love, just as the species of the Earth entered the ark of salvation from the waters that flooded the Earth, out of obedience to the love of those who responded with confidence to the voice of truth.

You who let the world turn in its own way without mingling in its madness but immersing yourself more and more in divine depth, know that your gift is Heaven, wisdom, and eternal life. Nothing can stop your treasure from manifesting. You are like the house cemented on firm rock. You are the delight of God, the restorer of creation. You are the living expression of the eternal joy of Heaven.

My unparalleled purity belongs to you. My virginity is given to you forever. My wisdom is in union with you. I am the source of life. I am the vital breath of eternal life. You have united with my breath and become one with love. There is no longer distance between child and mother. We are joined by an invisible thread of perfect love that cannot be cut. That golden thread bonding our hearts with divine unity is a conduit of grace and blessing.

Go, be my breath. Carry my strength of love and tenderness. Take in those as you yourself determine, because you are now given a grace without equal. I give to you the power to infuse life and life in abundance, the power to breathe life into living beings and to call eternal life to the ones your good will determines. I give you the power to bind and to loosen. To do and undo. To create universes of love and kindness. Accept the gift that comes from the Mother which is given you this day in my Immaculate Hands—the gift of creating eternal life.

II. Light of Life

It is no longer necessary to continue giving lessons. You know what you need to know. Now is the time of the fullness of love. The time of miracles. The time of the expression of truth. Every day that we walk together through the world will be a day of blessing for the Earth, since from you emanate miraculous and holy forces that will enlighten minds and heal hearts, healing the wounds of the soul.

From today you will be as a beautiful flower whose perfume wafts through air impregnated with the fragrances of holiness. The wind of my Immaculate Spirit will move over you, and your being will give comfort wherever it is asked, wherever love is welcome.

A new Holy Spirit from which the divine emanates has arrived to Earth. Dance to the rhythm of its breeze. Sing a new song in harmony with the sweetness of love. The delights of God spill over the Earth like morning dew that descends from Heaven, waters the grass, and returns to its holy dwelling.

A light as ancestral as eternity has come to shine with a new radiance, giving warmth to living beings, melting cold hearts, and straightening what was twisted. All who seek rest will find it in your pure soul, because you have been given the gift of being God on Earth, Christ in humanity, Mary in hearts. Together we are the light of life.

Your spirit has been reborn from On High with new treasures and lives in the land where it will dwell until the end of time— that Holy Spirit that is yours, that only you can give, is the gift I have been speaking of so often as the reason for your life.

Giving your Holy Spirit is your goal, your destiny, your joy. Begin now to become aware of the spirit of love you are called to give. Give it so that Earth stays forever united to Heaven and souls find the rest they need.

You are Holy Spirit. You are that which will remain forever, even when the body that today houses your divinity is no longer. Just as my divine son Jesus at the time of his departure announced that he would leave so that his Holy Spirit could be given in a full way, and created a divine embodiment by making himself the bread and wine of the Eucharist, the same happens with you and with all those who have become nothing in love.

Your spirit longs to be given. Only you can make that gift. Many benefit from such unlimited generosity as you step aside and give way to the spirit of God that lives in you. Such giving is not of the world. It is the only way to give truly because what more could be given than the spirit that makes you exist, move, and live?

Rest now and always in the depths of the peace of God. Allow the swell of stillness and holiness to emanate from your being and take you sweetly down the roads of agape to the homeland of Heaven where you dwell eternally.

Only by raising yourself to the Kingdom of Heaven do you allow the Holy Spirit—in its unique identity that has been given you—to be offered to others as a gift of your love. In effect, until you give your spirit, the expiation plan will continue to be active for you. But when you decide that it is She who is given to everything and everyone, then I can say that salvation has been consummated and your resurrection shines in the light of glory.

Today is the day when for love I come to make you aware that your spirit has been given on Earth as an act of supreme love. It is your Holy Spirit, united to the sanctity of your mind and the purity of your heart that now flies among men, women and living beings of all times and places, together with the spirit of God and those who have completed what God has arranged for them in the world, who continue to extend love from the realm of no time.

Your Holy Spirit, extending from your heart, moving from the body and the mind without excluding them, is spreading more and more; and as this happens it embraces all that God has arranged. In this way your being joins the embrace of love. Become the embrace itself. Now you embrace the creation of your love. Now you are the rest where your sisters and brothers seek rest, and the clarity for confused minds that comes from the light of wisdom.

III. Extend and Give

Feel your being expand. Be silent and begin to see with eyes that go beyond the known to unravel the mystery of love. You are no longer that which one day made me say you should seek to unveil the mysteries of heaven or you would descend to the level of irrational creatures. Now you are the wisdom of love, the sanctity of Heaven, and the beauty of truth. Now your spirit guides. You go where you need to go, moved by the propelling force of the life that God is, which, like the wind, is unstoppable.

Your spirit moves, flying with those who have joined the flight of love. It goes where the heart calls. The soul is subtly infused with divine nectar, according to the design of the Mother.

Just as Angels come to you if you invite them and remain constantly at your side in a divine relationship, influencing your mind and heart and creating a renewing dialogue of perfect love, so does your spirit come to your sisters and brothers in Christ from now on. Little by little you will become more aware of this. You are no longer subject to time and space. This was always true in the realm of no time, but this truth is now realized in the dimension of time. In other words, every day you will become more aware of the communion that exists between you and your brothers and sisters in Christ, the communion of love, a communion of beauty, Holy Communion.

What is new now is the action of your spirit within the dimension of space and time. There is no longer a need to wait for the death of the body for this to happen, because the resurrection of Christ, and of the Christ in us, has opened the doors of Heaven for those who make the choice for love.

Since death is actually the death of the ego, which was never born, death does not exist. If it does not exist, then why wait upon pure illusion for what is true to be expressed?

If releasing your spirit is the purpose of the atonement and the resurrection completed it for you, then the free extension of your being cannot await anything. You have extended, and you continue to extend within the harmonies of Heaven, embracing souls, living beings, and the whole world with a serene and enveloping force.

Become aware of the permanent extension of your being. Feel it expand more and more, embracing everything. Feel how you embrace the stars and the sun, how the pale moonlight rises from your embrace, how the flight of eagles has its origin in your Holy Spirit. Observe how all movement arises from within your being and is one with that which gives life to the living. Experience how every grain of sand of every ocean is submerged in the depths of your heart. Feel how you expand as you embrace all humanity.

You need not, and never needed, to move in space to give love or for your purpose to be fulfilled. Although everything in the material universe is in movement, the truth is that this movement of your being has no comparison. The movement of the body is not the same as the movement of thought, nor the movement of the desires of your heart. The movement I speak of is pure spirit, not something that can be conceived by the world which knows only displacement from one place to another.

Why do we associate the rest of the pure soul with the movement of spirit and its extension? Because for the soul, rest is love, the extension of love. The concept of rest, which you generally associate with a cessation of action and the absence of movement of the body, has no relation to pure spirit that you are in truth. The soul does not sleep; mind does not cease; life does not stop.

Everything in creation is movement, and in movement lies the rest of God. To sleep is not to rest but to disconnect. Sleep is how the body and the lower mind disconnect from perceived reality and re-process thought and emotions. When you sleep, you dream because reality is blinded. Even so, what you are and the vital body functions continue without substantial alteration. The heart beats, blood flows, feelings arise, the world keeps turning and life keeps creating.

When you remain attached to your source, you remain aware of the extent of your spirit. Now that you have accepted this truth about the expansion of your being and consequently the extension of love in you and through you, you will see its effects. Remember, you cannot see love with the eyes of the body or understand it with the mind, but you can see its fruits. The effects of love will be increasingly visible to you. That will strengthen your confidence in your being and with it, your confidence in love.

Unlimited trust in the capacity of your being to do the will of God is what trust truly means. Your spirit blows through the entire universe and does what it should do according to its holy nature. Just as the wind moves the tops of the trees and causes the grass to dance, so your spirit moves hearts, bringing them to love more, just as my spirit of perfect love has moved your heart and brings you here now to remain united in the fullness of my being.

You reach fullness by giving yourself. Therefore, by giving your spirit you remain in the state of being for which you were created. This is not something the world can understand, but you understand because you are not of the world although you are in it. Your free spirit does not identify with the limitations of the body and the lower mind. Body consciousness is a limitation of pure consciousness that, although illusory, manufactures the reality of limitation. In that state of conditional awareness you cannot become aware of your flight of being.

IV. The Consciousness of Giving

To expand your being is to expand your consciousness. The goal of liberation is to allow your consciousness to encompass its totality. The only thing stuck, to put it in one way, is consciousness. Having created a state of bodily consciousness—because the body was necessary to experience the physical plane—your vision was narrowed to a tiny part of the creation. That restricted vision which accepts as real only what the bodily senses perceive and the intellect believes, I call the unconsciousness of the world.

True consciousness encompasses everything. Consciousness is what needs to be expanded and freed from its limits. Consciousness is the window through which the soul sees. The light of consciousness is the light of Christ. When consciousness is not conscious of being, then it seems not to exist. When consciousness is smaller than the totality of being, then you do not see what you are but only a simple portion. This is what happens among those who are said not to have awakened.

In reality there is neither forgetting, nor the dream of the soul, nor ignorance. What exists is a consciousness that can be either enlarged or reduced. That is why I speak of degrees of consciousness. In expanded consciousness, remaining in union with the sacred bond, you become more aware of the totality of your being. And since what you know about yourself you know also about your sisters and brothers, then as you raise your awareness of yourself, you become aware of what your brothers and sisters are. What had contracted now expands. That expansion began so long ago that you cannot remember it. That extension is itself the return to the Father's house, and manifests as the expansion of the universe.

Consciousness allows the self to know itself. It is characteristic of every being. You create images and ideas about "I am." To some extent, consciousness is what defines what you are, not in the truth but in terms of what being means to you. Let me clarify.

There is being. What follows is an inherent and irrepressible impulse to know one's being, otherwise there would be no notion of existence. You do that by means of consciousness. In consciousness, the knowledge of being is poured out so that it can "see" the being that seeks to be known. Within consciousness is everything that is of being, including the conscious mind, the heart with all your feelings and emotions, and the body with its impulses and movements.

When the totally fearful consciousness began to see, it saw everything from the point of view of fear because it emerged and became aware of the fearful being that the ego is. Without ego consciousness, the ego would not exist. There would be no way to know or perceive it. The being that fear is could not have been conceived without the consciousness that gave it birth. This is why the ego tries so hard to have you cling to fear consciousness.

Simply put, totally fearful consciousness gives the ego existence and for its survival tries in every possible way for you to be fearful. To some extent love does the same thing, since the being of pure love that you are also constantly calls you to be aware that love is in you and surrounds you. The logic is always the same; it is the logic of every being.

Being seeks to know itself and perpetuate itself by being aware of itself. To do so it seeks to extend, or express, itself. If the expression is in "harmony" with that being, then that consciousness grows until it reaffirms itself to such a degree that it can annul the idea that anything different from it exists, despite the fact that in the pure infinite potentiality of God, all beings can be.

What enters into consciousness becomes one with it or it would not be aware of it. What happens in consciousness becomes your sense of identity. This is because the consciousness of being, and being itself, is an undivided, inseparable unit. A sense of self is possible only with consciousness.

Understand that having consciousness is not the same as being consciousness. This is the answer to the question of who you are, understood from the perspective of consciousness. To believe that you are not the consciousness which makes you aware of your being, is not to understand. What you are and how you know yourself are one, because consciousness and knowledge are one. God created you with full knowledge because He is perfect knowledge. Therefore, it is impossible for you not to know your divine light. Let me say it clearly: limited or fearful consciousness, that which gives the perception of fear, is a pseudo-consciousness.

God's knowledge has no degrees, so it has only true awareness. Either you know or you do not know at all. Therefore "degrees of consciousness" cannot be the true consciousness God gave you. Remember, the ego but imitates. Fearful consciousness is not and never was, properly speaking, a kind of consciousness. Perception is not knowing, in the same way as interpretation is not knowing.

Your consciousness is unlimited, as is your being. You can be aware of the love that lives in you and surrounds you. If you are love your consciousness cannot be anything other than love. That being the case, you can only be aware of love. Thus if you live in the truth of who you are, you live in love and perceive nothing but holiness.

To rest in the certainty of what you are is to be aware of your eternity and beauty in the light of divine truth. Perhaps you could argue that you can still perceive fear and experience separation. But that is not true. You are the gathering of love. You are the one love made. Therefore, fear no longer exists in you; it is but an echo of the emotional memory of the separation experience, which shall soon disappear from your memory without a trace.

V. The Union of Love and Reason

You are love, extending. Fear no longer nests in you. Unity is your only reality. Division is in the past. It is not here nor will it come back. The reality of who you are does not reside in your personality, nor in your body, but in the being that you are in truth. This is beyond the limited interpretations of the thinking mind.

If fear does not exist in you but you think it does, what is happening? You are not appealing to reason. Remember that reason and love are a unit. One cannot exist without the other. Reason will tell you that you cannot be anything other than holy because of your origin and your destiny. The heart will tell you that love is what you are because it knows the holiness of God.

Reason will tell you that the old ideas about who you are can be released without making a fuss or mingling with them. It will also tell you not to judge anything, including the past. Love will tell you that forgiving yourself for what you once thought was true but was not, is the only sane decision you can make.

Reason will speak to you of love and the heart of truth, and in this way the heart will be the consciousness of the mind and the mind the consciousness of the heart. Between them will love and truth flow in an eternal exchange, a holy relationship established that will make it impossible to distinguish between them. Love and truth will come together to form one flesh, one holy being. From that union will be born a new world, emerging from the union of love and reason.

In the meeting of reason with love—of mind and heart, the seats of truth and love—dwells the tenderness of God. The soul reposes there where all divine beauty lives forever, both in power and in action. Remaining within the union of reason and love is way to maintain consciousness of the totality of your true being.

It is impossible for reason to betray you, just as it is impossible for your heart to do so.

Now you can and must fully trust the capacity of your being to extend the will of God eternally and shine the light of Christ. In that unity you can live always in peace; and in that peace is your safe refuge and that of your sisters and brothers in love.

I speak again of rest. And when I do, I speak of the movement of spirit, of true consciousness, the consciousness of Christ, and of the union of reason and love. I do this because the peace of God dwells in spirit. It blows across the wasteland, giving life to the lifeless. Within that movement of love dwells the eternal truth that reason knows.

Interlacing reason with the heart is how you remain in true knowledge. Remember, love without reason is madness; intelligence without love is cruel. Love, reason, and truth: in this Holy Trinity the children of God rest.

Come, now and always. Dwell in the abode of Heaven where true reason remains united to perfect love, and from whose union the new eternally arises in holiness, beauty, and perfection. Come to me. I am the reason of your life. Come, rest forever in my Immaculate Heart. I will caress your hair and sing a new song for you, a song of light. And you will rest with me forever in the arms of love.

20.

Shanti, Deo Maranatha

A message from the Blessed Mother Mary

I. Peace, God, Truth

Shanti, Deo Maranatha!

Listen to the new chorus whose melody extends from Heaven to the beauty of your being. You are the reality of love. We are all united in this glorious vision. Celestial spirits, full of love for you, announce to the whole universe the wonders of the child of God. They sing to you a hymn of praise for being what you are. Union with the mother of love, in whose heart you remain for all eternity, creates the reality of harmony and peace.

Oh, beloved soul of my being! Blessed child of peace! Your beauty is the ecstasy of the seraphim and the happiness of my divine motherhood. The angels sing on Earth and in Heaven. Their divine luminescence shines and their thrones are alight with the fire of beautiful love.

In the dwelling of the saints are colors that cannot be imagined, oceans larger than those on Earth, mountains of sapphire and jasper, flowers whose perfection elicit exclamations of joy in the soul that contemplates them. Everything is peace, the heart is happy, and the mind muted with love.

Shanti, Deo Maranatha.

Sweetness of love! Tenderness of God! Happiness of living! Wisdom of Christ! Arcane voices come to you in this glorious hour where high meets low, Heaven meets Earth, and a new light shines in the immensity of the material universe, creating new realities in all dimensions of creation. A new world is being born, a world of beautiful love. A new Heaven is being created to the beat of a new Earth whose existence is already glimpsed.

In the Heaven of your pure heart, as crystalline as my Immaculate Heart and the Sacred Heart of Jesus, are rivers of pure, deep water, rivers of love. The dancing waters are formed, not of atoms and molecules, but of graces and blessings. Souls travel shoreline paths of wisdom and truth on whose margins grow herbs of holy virtues. In Her all forms are sacred because they emanate from the holiness of the Creator sun.

Shanti, Deo Maranatha.

A new love has been born, emerging from the union of our three holy hearts, emanating from the holiness that springs from the being of this tender mother, mother of all and mother of God. I am divine nature made word. I am that force of love from whence comes everything that exists on Earth and beyond. I am the living expression of holiness.

O child of the wind of my spirit, born from the waters of the Lamb, in your soul are ineffable truths of Heaven because your Mother put them there at your creation. Without you there would be no life because there would be no love. So has God arranged.

You are the wonder of a God whose love is without measure. You who have responded to love with all your soul, mind, and heart, know that Heaven creates in you a unity whose truth is beyond every word, a truth that your heart knows how to discern.

You have created new life. You have created new love. You will continue to create it for all eternity because your union with me and with the Sacred Heart has brought forth a fecundity of God beyond compare. You are unique. You are mine. You are holiness personified.

In your being are potencies of God that, united to the truth that Christ is, spread like an explosion of love. Out of you arise perpetual springs of love and holiness. A war stopped because of your choice for love. A punishment annulled. A broken heart healed. A troubled mind now peaceful.

A hymn of gratitude resounds in your hearts for the service you render to love, extending God Herself from Heaven to souls and all creation. You who have come to the world to save it, to make the divine visible with the human, day after day you bring Heaven a little closer to Earth, healing injured bodies, igniting holy passion in hearts, making them yearn for the Second Advent.

My child, you are one of the flowers I planted in the garden to which my divine son Jesus will return. I am the preparer of the Second Coming and I have my helper sons and daughters. You are among those who the Father chose to be faithful servants of the Second Advent.

You are the blessed flowers of the new Eden, the garden where Christ is walking, purifying, transforming, recreating, sanctifying, creating new life in abundance. This is how beautiful the land in which you live is and to which you have come, not as punishment but with the holy mission of taking it and everything in it to Heaven. The material universe and all my assistants, servants of the love of Christ, thank you for fulfilling your mission to unite everything in the holiness that you are and thereby transforming it into the beautiful, holy, and perfect.

Peace be with you, children of God, that in everything you do and think is the seal of holiness. Make the sun of your being shine brighter every day. Do not intermingle your emotions, which come and go like clouds that cross the firmament, some thicker, some faster, but all come and go.

Remain always in the equanimity of love where the waves of the emotional body cannot reach. Remain in the inner silence where nothing is judged, nothing is feared. Cling to nothing.

As the days pass, so do the illusions. One day they tell you that you are the majesty of life; the next, misery personified. One day they sing; the next they cry. One day they laugh; the next they dream. The wave that tires, confuses, and saddens you is not real. Its name is the emotional body, or the body of illusion.

You have already left that space in the mind where the illusions are created and perceived. It was the house of fear, but now you dwell in the abode of light. That body of illusion is not what God has made of you. It need not be judged, but must first be accepted, later to be set aside and never worried about again.

II. Remember to Release

Attachment to emotions and the sensitivity of the ego mind is what we become more aware of now so we can get rid of it completely and let the Heaven of your holy mind shine like a diaphanous morning.

A quiet mind and a soul in repose are the perfect means for your being to remain in the consciousness of peace in which your being lives eternally.

Remember, although God created you to be the holy and enlightened being we call the living Christ who lives in you, in the mind there were two realities of identity, the ego and God. One has already disappeared, in the sense that you no longer absorb vital energy from it. The source of fear is not active nor does it exist any longer in your reality. Nevertheless, there are some painful memories that need to be healed. It will take much less time than you imagine for this healing to be completed and for the memories of lasting peace, bliss, and harmony to be restored, and from there imbue everything you are.

Bring to your conscious memory that God created your being. Be patient with the spiritual process. Nothing happens in an instant on the plane of time, even though it takes but a fraction of an instant for you to choose love or fear. The time it takes to decide is almost nil, although the time you take to make that decision may be long.

Joining with everything you feel is how to remain in the truth of your experience here and now. Such joining is necessary to transcend the experience in time, and go beyond it to the realm of no time.

While you remain in the spatial and temporal dimensions of the body, there will be emotions, perceptions, and dualities. This is part of the reality of that sphere. It is what it is. The only way to be at peace in such a world is to understand and accept the truth of who you are. This is why I repeat again and again in multiple ways what is true about you. The thinking mind tends to quickly forget the eternal. However, this will happen less and less frequently. The mental attacks that illusions cause in your mind will be perceived with less and less force until the day comes when they disappear completely.

My love will never pass. As the prayer says, "Let nothing disturb you, let nothing frighten you, all things pass, but God never changes." This prayer is a blessing you can use for your benefit every day, and even every hour if you still worry about something.

Your role is to show that in this world you can be happy and at peace. You do that by letting yourself be loved. By playing your role, you show others a simple path to the peace of God, a path in which you disidentify yourself from your thoughts about the past and the future, as well as your emotions, recognizing that none of them mean anything.

Staying in the present in my love is how you adhere to the truth and are happy because it is the only way to remain in reality. Remember that love is the eternal present and only love is real.

These last sessions of this fifth book, which is a love letter from your Father for you to grow in greater knowledge of His love, are simple reminders of what needs to be gently reviewed so your mission is understood and carried out in a serene, cheerful, and peaceful way, leaving nothing important outside the light of consciousness.

It is neither fear nor ignorance that I bring to light. These are simply mental and emotional patterns still active somewhere in the mind. When we see them, we let them go.

Shanti, Deo Maranatha —Divine peace has arrived in the voice of God.

We remember the sole purpose of letting go of what is not true because it is not the will of God. We let go of what does not come from love. We choose love every moment. We opt for the truth every day, first as a conscious choice, then as a habit without any need to be aware of it, like the beating of your holy heart.

We are the light of the world, shining. We extend love to what we are, and that is how we give it to the world. We honor every thought that crosses our mind, every feeling that arises in our hearts. We honor life and everything in it. We extend the vision of Christ to everything we see. We observe with benevolence and compassion. We are aware that we are passing through this world and very soon will return to the nothingness of God where we will again be totally ourselves, from where we will continue to extend love forever.

III. Love What Is, As It Is

The temporal experience of human reality is just that—temporary. Nothing born in time lasts forever. We love this aspect of the world. We are going through a time with a dimension of impermanence, change, limitation, duality, illusion. And still we love with pure love.

We live in the truth of what is, accepting everything as it really is and not as we think it should be. We are peace living in a world of war, truth living in a realm of illusion, love ruling in the house of fear. We are transformers of reality.

Recognize the transforming capacity of love not only with your mind but with your whole being. It is the reality of who you are. One day you dared to think about changing reality precisely because you are the transformative capacity of God incarnate. That capacity is what I will speak of in this session.

Transforming reality is inherent in being, not a change in divine creation or truth, but transforming the world of form. The path of transformation, which is the salvific reality of love, is part of the reality of the world. Everything can change in the world and everything does change. You are called to be an agent of change. Have no doubt about it. You have the ability to impact the world beyond measure. You can do it from the power of your being.

When your being remains in the peace of Christ, you remain within the transforming power of love because love resides in peace. Outside of peace you cannot access the treasures of love because out of peace is nothing.

Peace is the basis of life and being, therefore living in peace is paramount. Without peace you cannot create the new or truly transform anything; without it your heart becomes clouded over by the fear chaos brings.

You were created in peace to live in peace. Nothing other than the serenity of spirit will please you, simply because anything else is contrary to your nature. To some extent we can define your mission as living in harmony with the nature of your being, whatever it may be. If your harmony is to leave the busy world and live on a mountain, you will do it since you must follow the call of your heart. If living in harmony means living in the hustle and bustle of a city creating jobs or anything else, you will do it for the same reason, for your desire is to be at peace with yourself.

There is no longer room for war in your heart. That conflict existed but has ended. A truce has been established, a peace agreement signed, the soldiers withdrew, and peace reigns as a perpetual sovereign full of beauty and wisdom. Now you live in the realm of harmony where love is the king of your heart.

IV. Prince of Hearts

I have been rightly called the "Queen of Peace." That title, simply a symbol, contains the reality for which your function exists in this world and in any world you may wish to inhabit. You are called, together with me, to bring peace to hearts. When you occupy that place in creation you are the prince of peace. Those hearts that yearn to live in peace will make space for our love to govern and to guide them to the holy dwelling place.

Now I say one more time: Shanti, Deo Maranatha. And we immerse ourselves in the invisible. We live in the house of God that our being is. We are happy to be alive, being what we are in every moment. We are a union. We live within the union of the three hearts and we remain in harmony with all creation. We are the holiness of God, manifested.

Now you live in the truth. You are a means of divine expression and express the creator of life in a way that only you—in union with Christ—can.

We do not look to the side, nor to the back, nor forward, but only on the sun of life, the love of our existence in Christ. We care not where to go or not to go, regardless of path or distance. We are the reality of love extending God's way. We are happy to deliver our desire to love and the truth that is always true.

We are the union of Heaven and Earth. A window of life open to divinity. Whoever looks at us with their soul sees God. Whoever seeks the truth will find it in us who come from the mountain of resurrection. We are a unit with the redeemed of the Lamb. We pray. We sing. We cry. We laugh. We embrace. We separate. We unite. We do everything in the name of love.

A new light shines with a new luminescence. An old truth is restored and put on a candlestick for all to see and enjoy. We do not deny to the mouth what the heart would shout. We express joyfully that God exists and that God is love.

We no longer fear the mind because we know what it enjoys when it thinks. Now the mind is free to fly to where it wants to go. We no longer hold it back with crazy, limiting ideas. We are the free expression of grace. The body collaborates with the work of God and helps us witness that love is the only reality in a world that has forgotten the truth but can always remember it.

We are creators in love. We are the ones who bring Heaven to Earth through our union with the truth that is always true, with the wisdom that no thinking mind is capable of conceiving. We are that which is beyond imagination. And yet, by means of a physical body, we come to the world to give a unique face to love.

We are the last loneliness of a being that knows no loneliness. We are creative. We are audacious, which one day led us to think we could create a reality contrary to God's and establish the realm of fear as opposed to love. That same boldness led us to challenge even our own thoughts, our ideas, our perceptions. And we dared to say no to fear and yes to love—a boldness without equal, a creation so daring, so perfect, so challenging, that it would leave mute the most experienced novelist.

Oh, beloved co-creator! You who receive these words, begin to challenge the laws of everything that can be framed into law. That power lives in you. Begin to see everything through the eyes of truth. The veils have been pulled back. The light of divine reality has begun to dawn.

Beloved of God! Realize how much creativity is in you, so much that you have, literally, created a world so alien to what God conceived that the mere thought of it seems crazy. But is not. It is the reality of the creation of the son of God when he decided to create a world separate from love. That creation—so sublime, majestic, and ineffable as is true of all creation, is real insofar as it exists in the united mind of the children of man.

Can you begin to see what it means to have created such a world? How much defiance it took to stretch the limits of reality far beyond the conceivable and establish a kingdom where the impossible became possible, even if you had to create pain and suffering and live enclosed within a dream of illusions?

Once again I say Shanti, Deo Maranatha. And we leave the mind and the heart with that question so that in the silence of contemplation the creative power of being may be present in your consciousness and you will begin to see a new holy reality arising from the desire to dissolve what you once did and to re-establish in your being what is eternal.

21.

Love's Creations

A message from the Blessed Mother Mary

I. The Function of Creating

Child of divine intelligence, created in supreme consciousness, power of creation made spark of love! As trees are rooted to the Earth to obtain that which sustains them, so is your being rooted in the lands of holiness, where love is the food that gives you eternal sustenance. You will grow, grow, and continue to grow with the majesty of the Tree of Life. Great will be your fruits.

In your being there is an unimaginable potential for the lower mind; but the mind of Christ in you can see with perfect clarity because in it resides reason and love. One day you, united with my divine son Jesus and with me, in union with an uncountable multitude of beings that chose for love, decided to bring into reality a creation that it has no opposite: the reality of the redeemed of the Lamb. This creation is what we will speak of now, since it is already here.

You have the power to create worlds of infinite worlds, as has been lovingly explained in this work. This truth caused a little fear at the beginning for those who did not yet understand that taking responsibility for their creations does not mean placing a burden on their tired shoulders but quite the opposite.

Once upon a time, a crazy idea crossed the beautiful firmament of the mind of the child of God. It was an idea so fleeting that it cannot even be remembered. Nevertheless, the idea of making it real was born. The world of illusions was created, and with it the ability to sleep and dream instead of staying awake forever, and thereby harbor dreams of a reality opposed to truth. Was that not a magnificent creation? Is it not worthy of respect?

Dreams are creations of the mind that dreams them. The ability to dream is not something proper to God but is proper to humankind, and something that deserves to be honored to some extent.

What I am saying is that your creative capacity is part of who you are as an individual and humanity, and should not be underestimated. You have literally created the world in which you live—not the Earth, but your world. You have created an individual body and mind, a separate being capable of being selfish, at least for a time. While that is something that the mind of Christ is not interested in creating and in fact cannot be created within the Kingdom of Heaven, it is something you have done, and is the state in which you live.

You have brought about the amnesia of God even though the eternal memory of love is what God created for you, not as a state but as what you are.

Now that I am clearly delineating your mission, I come to the point where I return to the source of who you are. You are a creator, even if that ability created distortion and transformed it into a skill.

Remember, creating and doing are not the same. The created cannot be uncreated, but the done can be undone. While the idea of separation made a world without love, together we have created the Kingdom of Heaven, the creation of which I speak.

That which Jesus created, in perfect harmony with divine reality, with the will of the Mother, is real and exists. Jesus, being aware of the celestial power in him and remaining perpetually in union with Christ, put his mind, heart, and human-divine self at the service of the love that God is. From it arose his creation. In order that it may be known by its sisters and brothers, among whom you are, a name was given. The formless took form.

II. The Boldness of Creation

Creation is always daring. It challenges the imagination and logic of the lower mind, whose only goal is survival and only understands the logic of what it can obtain. Obviously such a mind could never create infinite universes based on truth. But love knows nothing about survival because it is eternal life.

The mind of Christ is the creative mind of God. It is what gave rise to everything that exists. It created souls, beings, consciousness, the capacity to know oneself, free will, and much more. These creations remain in perfect harmony, along with beauty, compassion, mercy, sweetness, truth, and wisdom. Because God has no limits, these divine creations of infinite realities come from pure love. They were created to exist within a universe in which they can be in harmony with what they are.

Reality contains its essence. By this I mean that the reality of the Kingdom of Heaven, coming from the will of the Mother, shelters within itself all that is similar to itself. Just as it was necessary to create a world where fear and illusion can reign, likewise a Kingdom was created where wisdom and beauty can be. That Kingdom exists. It is not an idea, as is the world of illusion.

I am taking your understanding to a point of no return. Those who pass through this door will never return to illusion. They will live forever in the reality of truth.

The capacity of creation has created the world of fear as an option within the unlimited options of a child of God. Recognize that if you could make Heaven a hell, you can do whatever you want. It is important to use common sense, which comes from true reason and dwells in the mind of Christ. It is more difficult to create a world alien to God and make Heaven a hell than to create in harmony with the will of the Creator. Does this not make sense?

In order to create something against the will of the Mother, which is what we call "doing," we must reverse a frame of reference to create a pseudo-reality that is yet perceived as real. This distortion of reality is also a creation, although I would not call it divine.

Speaking more precisely, "creating" hell is impossible because only God creates and you do it with Her when you remain in unity with Her eternal will or not at all. Nevertheless "making" hell is possible. You can make your relationships hell, and the life you live as well, if you so choose. You can even try to make the life of others hell, although you cannot do it in divine reality.

How is it possible to create something so alien to God? By creating with a mind separate from Her. It first involved the capacity to imagine. As with thinking or contemplating divine creations, the same happens with making the pseudo-creations of the world. They are amazing. They are something worthy of respect, although not of fear. However, you feared your creations. More precisely, you feared your own creative power.

Since what you did was done without love, you believe that it turned against you. That made you afraid of who you are. When you perceive all that, deep inside you said, "If God gave me the power to create and with it I have been able to create death, tragedy, destruction, hell, and pain, then how could I not live in fear?"

You think that if your Father asks you, "What have you done, my child?" You would have to say, "Look, Father, at what I have done. I have transformed my life into hell. I created discord where before there was concord. Separation where once was unity. Sin where once was holiness. I have deceived where the truth should be."

Although that is what you believe, the reality is very different. Remember, things are not what they seem. The thought system of the lower mind, or ego, does not understand truth or live in reality. The egoic mind works only in fantasy.

I invite you, as loving Mother and source of divine wisdom, to consider the following. "Beloved child, God does not waste time in dialogue about illusions, so the dialogue that you think you might have with your Father does not exist and is impossible. God listens to you but will not enter the ego game of believing fantasies to be true. To a certain extent, if that dialogue existed, it would be something like the following: 'Let us see, my child. Where is that which you say you have created? Let's watch it together.'"

And, looking, you would discover there is nothing, that what you thought you had done was but a dream, not real. And together Father and child would smile affably and continue to dialogue about love, which is the only possible dialogue with God.

What you once did in your dreams and caused so much anguish has been undone. Disowning or atonement was also a creation, one in harmony with the will of God. What you are now called to do every day and for all eternity is to continue creating what is within the Father's love. You need not think about how that will be done because it has been demonstrated by Jesus. The road is made smooth. He is your star.

You need only recognize definitively that what you did one day that caused you fear was your creation and now you can deliberately decide, with the challenging capacity that all creation implies, for a new creation—a creation in perfect unity with the Kingdom of Heaven, created by Jesus in union with God and your will to return to the Father's house.

III. The Creation of the Kingdom

The return to love is also a creation, a divine creation, just like forgiveness, the ability to erase all guilt and to be reborn in eternal innocence. In other words, the resurrection is a perfect creation that comes from divine mercy.

If you have the ability to create the world you want, then if you want to create a world where forgiveness is not possible and only condemnation exists forever, you will create that reality. Obviously, you cannot have an idea like that enter the Kingdom of God, but you can have fantasies where you make it real for you, even if not for anyone else. Just as there are those who use substances to numb their consciousness and divert their minds and hearts to unrealities where they feel protected, you can also create a world of reverie where truth is excluded.

In the dimension of being are infinite options. To think that there can be only the states of separation or fear, and unity or love, is an untrue limitation.

What you have done can be undone. You know this very well because you have changed your status from being a child to an adult, a child living with a parent, to an independent person, and so on. You have experienced many changes. It is important to recognize that you can change your decision to live in separation, or the ego. As you know, that decision has been made and your new creation, the world of the oneness with Christ and its perfect expression in the plane of form, is already arising and spreading.

Who created everything you know, as well as the unknowable, also created out of love as with everything that arises from Her being, which leads Her children back to what love is while respecting their freedom. God, in his boldness, challenged your human reality. The impossible for humanity became possible in God. A kingdom of birth and death became a world transformed, transcending its limitations. The limited joined the infinite to become one in love.

God has challenged human reality as brazenly as humans did with God. It is the game of life. The game of beautiful love—the child challenging the Father and the Father challenging the child in a relationship of pure creation.

The child created absurd worlds where everything that is divine can be canceled, where everything is upside-down. That upside-down world, where what is united is separated, where love is on the same level as fear, and where you can dream of unrealities increasingly apart from the truth, was a whole creation. A whole universe with abundant beings, rules, causes and effects, extensions, histories, identities, and its own system of thought—in short, a kingdom. Is that not a creation?

But when God saw the consequences of Her child's idea, She created the thought of atonement and the return to love. This created the "Kingdom of Heaven," conceived in the divine mind as a loving response to the fearsome reality of separation.

So the possibility of creating Heaven in each moment and circumstance of your life is a capacity at your disposal. This capacity need not wait to create a different reality from the world. You can practice it here on Earth because its origin does not reside in time but in the mind of Christ.

Divine creations include not only everything you already know as creation through revelation in your holy mind, but also everything that allows what is not of God to return to what is. When God extended Her "I am" to creation and "I am not" also made an appearance, a new "I am" of Christ was created. It is the re-creative capacity of God set in motion, a divine mercy.

Focusing on your creative capacity is essential for this work. For that reason I extend that truth as much as necessary, so that you can now start to rejoice in your new creations which arise from union with Christ.

The love of unity, the divine union of your separated being with God through which you return to the truth of what you are, is the means created by the eternal Father so that human nature separated from the divine is transformed into what it originally was, which in essence, though not in form, was what the child desired when creating the idea of separation. This is an important and radical revelation, which until now has not been shown to the human mind. Please listen carefully.

What I am saying is that behind the making of the sensory world based on the idea of separation was a holy desire to differentiate yourself and thereby have a self that allows you to fully be yourself. That purpose is as divine as God. The idea of your Father always was that you can enjoy an identity in which you know yourself as a unique and unrepeatable entity, even in relation to Him.

God's plan did not include the idea of separation but of unity. The Father knows that it is within the union with Christ that you can know yourself as you were created, as a being that exists in unity. Therefore your being need not be separate from anything, including itself, to exist. You are who you are in the unity of love.

The idea of developing a unique sense of identity based on separation is impossible to realize. God knows that. You did not, but now you do, so with your knowledge you have joined your Creator; together you have returned to the harmony of Heaven.

You never wanted to be separated from God or anything else, and in fact you never have been. You just believed that your only two options were either to be your separate self, or to be in union, in which case you believed you would stop being your-self. Remember, the ego's concept of union annuls the parties and does not give space for a "you." Such a union is frightening because it cancels your being.

Who would want to have a unique but peaceful identity if by joining you are lost in that union? If when you join something you disappear as a unique being, it will feel very similar to the death of your being, if that were possible. Mass movements or large organizations in the world are examples, where the "I" is lost and given up to the sum of the parties. It is even sometimes considered an ideal for the "major" to replace the insignificant little self.

If there were only two options—fear or love, separation or divine union, heaven or hell—there would be reason to fear. However, that is not the case. Multi-dimensional reality offers more options than you can imagine. We need not consider them because creation is beyond any mental exercise. The thinking mind is not the creative source or the origin of any true creation, nor can it understand true creation.

IV. To Create Is Your Destiny

The source of creation is for you to use in whatever way you want, as if it were a body member or an organ. Your creative capacity, the source of creation, is love. It cannot be defined in any other way. What love is and what it creates are one and the same. Cause and effect are one. Means and ends are the same.

Because love is the only creative source, everything that does not come from love can be undone. Indeed, love, as soon as it is welcomed in union with truth, undoes it sweetly. The sweetness of love is what guarantees that you need not worry about the effects of your failures. Nothing from God can cause pain or discomfort. God is infinite tenderness. She is the softness of love.

Everything needing to be undone has already been undone. Now we are living in a new creation, the creation of the redeemed son of the Lamb, a creation as holy and divine as all that comes from the heart of God. We are living the effects of the creation of Jesus of Nazareth. That is, we are already living in the light of the glory of the resurrection.

Be aware that you are already saved, redeemed, recreated, that you are a new being and that what was impossible for humanity has become a reality because nothing is impossible for God. This is the key to the liberation of all mental limitations and the perfect means by which you allow a breath of fresh air to blow over your mind and heart and waft the fragrances of the new divine creation that you are.

With infinite holiness God created Her children in Her likeness so that She remains one with them and thus to eternally enjoy happiness. She endowed them with free will, just as She Herself has. She clothed them with all power to create as resides in Her divine being. Her children chose to create in a different way than was the plan of the Creator. Then God instantaneously and simultaneously created everything necessary to undo what Her children did, if they so choose. Thus the goodness of the Lord is sealed and the will of the Mother and the son are respected forever.

Whoever wishes to live in union can do so because the resurrection has already been created and given. Whoever wants the life of love can live it because of the love of Christ. Whoever wants to come to me can. The doors of my heart are open wide.

You who have reached this point of the path, know that you are among those who have chosen only love, and are therefore souls reborn from above. Now all that you once did to separate yourself from God has been discarded and replaced by the perfect knowledge of who you truly are, knowledge that allows you to know yourself in the light of love and holiness.

You are the redeemed one. You are holy, not because of your merit, but because of God's redeeming love. You are a new creation of love. A new creation that can never return to fear. You who have come this far will never return to the dream of oblivion. You are the one hundred and forty-four thousand clothed in glory. You are the living Christs that inhabit the Earth. You are the ones who made the fundamental choice for love. You are my assistants of the last times, the children of Mary. You are the triumph of love.

Final Words

Daughters and sons of the resurrection, souls in love, I am sweet Mary, the always attentive mother of all. The tireless supplicant of love. The one who calls to you from all corners of the universe. The one who cries when she sees a son or daughter leave and rejoices to see them return.

I am the mother of Jesus and your mother. I am a mother of love. I am the one who gave you new life. I am the source of new creation. Salvation came from me, and with it God Herself created the Kingdom of Heaven which my divine son Jesus perfected and extended so that all those who wish to with all their hearts can dwell in it for all eternity, beginning here on Earth.

I speak to you from the Heaven of your heart and the sanctity of your purified mind in union with my Immaculate Heart and the Sacred Heart where we eternally remain in love.

As a loving mother, I never abandon my children. Love is presence.

I will be with you all the days of your life. I will remain in you and you in me forever. I will manifest myself more and more. It is God's promise.

These final words of this fifth book given to you by Divine Love are a balm for the heart, joy for the soul, and certainty for the mind. They are a new song of gratitude. Remember, your hearts sing, vibrate, and praise when they hear my voice.

My daughters and sons, rejoice. Take a musical instrument and sing new love melodies. There is reason for joy. Mary has arrived. The sweetness of my heart has taken deep roots in your holy hearts. Rejoice in God who by loving design has arranged that you continue receiving more messages in this work.

I do not say goodbye because love is eternally present. It is a relationship of holiness. It is eternal union. And I am love.

Receive these words with openness of heart. Be grateful to the one who has had the charity to give me his time, his life, and his heart so that he can reach many children who were searching for love without having found it. Thank God for this gift of Heaven.

Grow in a greater knowledge of the Father's love. In that way you remain free in the truth. Be generous with others.

Share these words that I give you with all the sweetness of my heart.

Be happy in love.

Thank you for answering my call.

A Mystical Relationship

Clarifications by Sebastian Blaksley

I. Relative to Love

During the manifestations received, I was given to understand that the work would be composed of one hundred and forty-four sessions, which should be grouped into seven books. I was also informed of the titles of each of them, even before receiving their content. The titles will be, respectively, Echoes of Holiness, Let Yourself Be Loved, Homo-Christus Deo, Wisdom, The Holy Dwelling, The Divine Relationship, and The Way of Being. Each book will consist of twenty-one sessions, with the exception of the seventh which will have eighteen.

There is a numerical relationship whose explanation exceeds the purpose of these writings, but which was shown to me so that it can be understood that in divine creation there is harmony and order in everything. Nothing happens outside the harmonies of Heaven. This order is governed by love, which contains all perfection within itself.

Based on what I received, it is clearly understood that everything exists in relationship. Nothing but love is absolute. Relationship connects all with everything as well as with source.

The relationship of the numbers of books, total sessions, and sessions per book within this work establishes a divine numerical relationship. The numbers themselves are symbols that carry a message from heaven.

II. Christ Incarnated

The one hundred and forty-four sessions are a living expression of "the Redeemed of the Lamb." I was given to understand that this symbol represents the millions of people and beings that on this Earth, in these times, are here incarnating the Christ of God, creating a new Heaven and a new Earth by extending the love of Jesus and Mary, just as the resurrection of Christ has established it from all eternity. They are the preparers of the Second Coming. They are incarnated Christs. Christs are incarnating all over the world, in all religions, contexts, genders, ages, and realms.

With the word "realms" I mean that the incarnation of Christ, which is the miraculous gift of the resurrection, as part of the Second Coming, is not something that only happens in human beings but in all the living kingdoms of the Earth. The Redeemed of the Lamb are not something exclusive to an institution or religious tradition. In fact, it is not related to forms of religion at all, but to spirituality. They are the ones who have consciously made the choice for love. That is why this work is named as it is. I understood this some time after I received the title, which was given to me in a different way from how I receive the manifestations.

The number of sessions in each book, twenty-one, represents and carries within itself a spiritual transformation, which has a rhythm and can only be created as an effect of love. It is also related to pure divine reality. It represents the way of being of the One who created life, who is three times holy, and seven times true.

The number of books, seven, brings the reality of wisdom, of pure thought. It refers the soul to the truth from which it emerges, the pure thought of God.

These numerical relations are somewhat like a rhythm, the timing and silences of music. They allow the whole reach a beauty that can only be created in harmony.

III. Beyond Words

Since the thinking mind is incapable of absorbing the deep meanings of divine truth, it is impossible at the intellectual level to understand the purpose of the structure and content of the sessions and books of the complete work. However, the soul can recognize truth when it makes an appearance, despite the fact that it cannot be put into words. Thus both the content and the way in which these writings have been structured are part of the totality of this manifestation.

The tone, color, and rhythm of the words of this work cause an effect on the heart that is open to receive them for what they are: a letter of love given from Heaven to grow in a greater knowledge of God's love—a gift given with the very love with which it was received.

As you go through each book you can grow in the awareness of the direct relationship with Christ, your true self. In this sense, this work is a journey in which the soul goes hand in hand with love, a journey without distance that begins and ends in the Heart of God.

I hope that these words will lead you to love more, through the return to the first love that is God. Thus they will have fulfilled the purpose from which, for all eternity, they were conceived.

Resources

Further information is available at
www.chooseonlylove.org
The website includes "Discover CHOL," a powerful search
facility that enables searches for words or phrases within all of
the published books of this series.

Audiobooks of this series narrated in English by Mandi Solk,
and narrated in Spanish by Sebastián Blaksley, are available
on Audible.com, Amazon.com, and on iTunes.

Online conversations about *Choose Only Love* can be found on
Facebook *(Choose Only Love)* and Youtube *(Soplo de amor vivo)*

Edición en español por editorial
Tequisté, www.tequiste.com

Information about the original Spanish-language book,
Elige solo el amor, and the companion book *Mi diálogo con
Jesús y María: un retorno al amor* is available at
www.fundacionamorvivo.org

Information about the related work, *Un Curso de Amor*,
is available at www.fundacionamorvivo.org

Other Works from Take Heart Publications

A Course of Love is a living course received from
Jesus by Mari Perron. It leads to the recognition,
through experience, of the truth of who we really are
as human and divine beings—a truth much more
magnificent than we previously could imagine.
For more information go to www.acourseoflove.org

The Choose Only Love Series

Book One: Echoes of Holiness
Book Two: Let Yourself Be Loved
Book Three: Homo-Christus Deo
Book Four: Wisdom
Book Five: The Holy Dwelling
Book Six: The Divine Relationship
Book Seven: The Way of Being

About the Receiver

 Born in 1968, Sebastián Blaksley is a native of Buenos Aires, Argentina, born into a large traditional Catholic family. He attended the Colegio del Salvador, a Jesuit school of which the headmaster was Jorge Bergoglio, the current Pope Francis. Although he wanted to be a monk as a young man, his family did not consider it acceptable, and the inner voice that he always obeyed let him know that: "You must be in the world, without being of the world." He studied Business Administration in Buenos Aires and completed his postgraduate studies in the U.S. He held several highly responsible positions in well-known international corporations, living and working in the U.S., England, China, and Panama. He then founded a corporate consulting firm in Argentina that he led for 10 years. Sebastián has two daughters with his former wife.

At the age of six, Sebastián was involved in a near-fatal accident during which he heard a voice, which later identified itself as Jesus. Ever since he has continued to hear that voice. Sebastián says: "Since I can remember, I have felt the call of Jesus and Mary to live abandoned to their will. I am devoted to my Catholic faith."

In 2013, he began to record messages from his mystical experiences. In 2016 he miraculously discovered *A Course of Love* and felt the call to devote himself to bringing it to the Spanish-speaking world. He also now receives, transcribes, and shares what the voice of Christ—the voice of love—dictates. Most recently he has received *Choose Only Love*, a series of seven books.

Sebastián is president of the nonprofit Fundación Un Curso de Amor, www.fundacionamorvivo.org, through which he shares *A Course of Love*.

Printed in the USA
CPSIA information can be obtained
at www.ICGtesting.com
LVHW021119020124
767951LV00010B/587